Jolly Phonics

Handbook

Written by

Sue Lloyd and Sara Wernham

Illustrated by Lib Stephen and
Yoana Gurriz Muñoz

Edited by Angela Hockley

Fourth Edition

Contents

Part 1: Introduction

Part 2: Reproducible Material

Reproducible Section 1

Learning the Letter Sounds and Letter Formation

Reproducible Section 2: Lesson Plans & Sound Sheets

Reproducible Section 3: Flashcard Sheets

Reproducible Section 4: Sound Book Sheets

Blending

Reproducible Section 5: Word Box Sheets

Suggested Timetable for Jolly Phonics: STEP 1

	Daily Teaching	Week 1	Week 2	Week 3	Week 4	Week 5	Week 6	Week 7	Week 8	Week 9+
Letter Sound Recognition	• Sound sheets and actions • Flashcards and games • Sound books • Jolly Phonics Wall Frieze • Jolly Songs	s a t i p	n c k e h r	m d g o u	l f b ai j	oa ie ee or z w	ng v oo oo y x	ch sh th qu ou	oi ue er ar	Continue to review the letter sounds.
		\-- • Introduce the sounds, letters, and actions through stories, at a rate of one sound a day. • Review the letters and sounds so that the students know them well. (Weeks 1–8) --\						\-- • Learn the sounds of the capital letters in preparation for reading sentences. --\		
Letter Formation	• Multisensory practice: - pencil hold - correct formation	\-- • Feel the letter shapes: air writing / grooved letters in the Finger Phonics books. • Learn the formation of the new letters. Review the formation of recently learned letters. • Practice neat letter formation: sound sheets, dry-wipe boards, lined paper. --\								
Blending (for reading)	• Hear the word after the sounds have been spoken by the: a) teacher b) students • Letter games / activities • Word boxes • Decodable readers	• Aural blending: the teacher says the sounds in a word / the students listen for the word.			\-- • Blend words with: - initial and final consonant blends, e.g. *stop* and *milk*. - double letters, e.g. *duck* and *hill*. --\		\-- • Start using word boxes and/or the JP Little Word Books with students who can independently blend simple regular words. --\			• Introduce decodable readers: - JP Readers, Orange Level for hesitant readers. - JP Readers, Red Level for confident readers.
			\-- • Frequently blend simple words that use the taught letter sounds, including words with digraphs. --\							
			\-- • Introduce the reading of phrases (Week 2) and simple sentences (Week 5), using suggestions from the lesson plans and/or JP Word Bank. Demonstrate how to "tweak" certain words, such as *a* and *is* to get the correct pronunciation. --\							
Identifying Sounds in Words (for writing)	• Segment regular words • Dictation	• Call out simple words, e.g. *dog, clap, sheep*.	\-- • Identify the sounds in a word: Is there a /s/ in *nest?* Is it at the beginning, the middle, or the end? The students respond by saying the individual sounds and holding up a finger for each one: /d-o-g/ (3 sounds, 3 fingers); /c-l-a-p/ (4 sounds, 4 fingers); /sh-ee-p/ (3 sounds, 3 fingers). Write the sounds on the board as they are called out and blend them with the students to read the word and check it is correct. • Dictate letter sounds and simple regular words, including words with digraphs. --\							
Tricky Words	• Read tricky words and identify the tricky part • Write tricky words, remembering how the tricky part is spelled.								• Teach the first 12 tricky words: /sh/ lesson: *I* /th/ lesson: *the* /qu/: *he, she* /ou/: *me, we* /oi/: *be* /ue/: *was* /er/: *to, do* /ar/: *are, all*.	• Continue to review the tricky words.

Suggested Timetable for Jolly Phonics: STEP 2

Weekly Units	1	2	3	4	5	6	7	8	9	10	11	12	13
Alternatives	⟨y⟩ as /ee/	short vowels	⟨ck⟩	double letters	long vowels and ⟨a_e⟩, ⟨e_e⟩, ⟨i_e⟩, ⟨o_e⟩, ⟨u_e⟩		⟨ay⟩ as /ai/, ⟨oy⟩ as /oi/	⟨ea⟩ as /ee/	⟨y⟩ and ⟨igh⟩ as /ie/	⟨ow⟩ as /oa/ and /ou/	⟨ir⟩ and ⟨ur⟩ as /er/	⟨ew⟩ as /ue/	⟨aw⟩, ⟨au⟩, ⟨al⟩ as /ol/

Alternatives:
- Use flashcards to review the 42 basic letter sounds, short and long vowels, and alternatives that have been taught.
- Use dictation to review the alternative spellings taught so far.
- Read words, phrases, and sentences as frequently as possible, and use blending for unknown words.
- Listen for the short and long vowels in words and introduce some of the spelling rules associated with them (e.g. using ⟨ck⟩ after a short vowel).

Weekly Units	1	2	3	4	5	6	7	8	9	10	11	12	13
Handwriting (top)	Capitals SATIPN	Capitals CKEH RMD	Capitals GOULFB	Capital J	Caps ZWV	Caps YXQ	Review the alphabet: upper- and lower-case letters	Review formation: • ⟨b⟩ & ⟨d⟩ • capitals A–M	Review: • ⟨r⟩, ⟨n⟩, ⟨m⟩, ⟨h⟩ • capitals N–Z	Review: • caterpillar ⟨c⟩ letters • alphabet order	Review: • tall letters • alphabet order	Review: • letters with tails under the line • alphabet	Review: • ⟨e⟩, ⟨z⟩, ⟨s⟩, ⟨v⟩, ⟨w⟩, ⟨x⟩ • alphabet order
Handwriting (bottom)				Review ⟨ai⟩, ⟨oa⟩, ⟨ie⟩, ⟨ee⟩, ⟨or⟩	Review capitals: Groups 1&2	Review capitals: Groups 3–7							

Handwriting:
- Practice correct letter formation for both upper- and lower-case letters.
- Introduce the letter names through reciting/singing the alphabet, starting in Unit 1.
- Review the lower-case letters and corresponding capitals that have been taught (Jolly Phonics Alphabet Poster / flashcards / upper- and lower-case letter matching / capital and word dictation).
- From Unit 7: Introduce the alphabet in four color-coded groups: A–E; F–M; N–S; T–Z. Each group represents roughly a quarter of the words in a dictionary.

Weekly Units	1	2	3	4	5	6	7	8	9	10	11	12	13
Words and Sentences	the hen	in the park	on the pond	the fox	the fish	in the dark	the noisy ducks	the queen	digging for gold	the shark in the ship	fixing the car	the statue	having a picnic

Discussion pictures for each lesson:
- Use pictures for discussion and vocabulary building.
- Model how to write words, phrases, and sentences with the students, including capital letters, periods, and spaces between words.
- Encourage independent writing about the pictures, using words, phrases, or sentences, according to ability.

Weekly Units	1	2	3	4	5	6	7	8	9	10	11	12	13
Tricky Words	you, your	come, some	said, here, there	they	go, no, so	my, one, by	only, old	like, have	live, give	little, down	what, when	why, where	who, which

Tricky Words:
- Read the tricky words and identify the part(s) that are tricky.
- Practice writing the tricky words by looking for the tricky part(s), copying the word, covering and writing it, then checking the spelling.
- Use flashcards and dictation to review reading and writing the tricky words that have been taught.
- From Unit 5, sufficient teaching has been covered to introduce the Jolly Phonics Readers, Yellow Level. Only give to confident readers at this stage.

Suggested Timetable for Jolly Phonics: STEP 3

Weekly Units

	1	2	3	4	5	6	7	8	9	10	11	12	13
Alternatives	⟨ph⟩ as /f/	soft ⟨c⟩	soft ⟨g⟩	Review the main alternative vowel spellings.					Review the main alternative vowel spellings.				
				⟨ai⟩, ⟨a_e⟩, ⟨ay⟩	⟨ee⟩, ⟨e_e⟩, ⟨ea⟩	⟨ie⟩, ⟨i_e⟩, ⟨y⟩, ⟨igh⟩	⟨oa⟩, ⟨o_e⟩, ⟨ow⟩	⟨ue⟩, ⟨u_e⟩, ⟨ew⟩ as /oo/	⟨ou⟩ and ⟨ow⟩	⟨oi⟩ and ⟨oy⟩	⟨er⟩, ⟨ir⟩, ⟨ur⟩	⟨aw⟩, ⟨au⟩, ⟨al⟩	⟨air⟩, ⟨ear⟩, ⟨are⟩ as /air/

Alternatives
- Use flashcards and dictation to review the alternative spellings that have been taught.
- Use the "vowel hand" regularly to review the short and long vowel sounds.
- Read words, phrases, and sentences as frequently as possible, and use blending for unknown words.
- Identify short and long vowels in words and reinforce the spelling rules associated with them (e.g. the alternative vowel spellings ⟨ay⟩ and ⟨oy⟩ are nearly always used at the end of a word).

	1	2	3	4	5	6	7	8	9	10	11	12	13
Read, Write, and Review	Review capital letters and the four color-coded alphabet groups.						Review letter formation and using digraphs in words and sentences.						
	ABCDE	FGHI	JKLM	NOPQRS	TUVW	XYZ	⟨oa⟩, ⟨ng⟩	⟨oo⟩, ⟨or⟩	⟨ie⟩, ⟨ee⟩, ⟨ue⟩	⟨sh⟩, ⟨ch⟩, ⟨th⟩	⟨er⟩, ⟨ar⟩, ⟨ai⟩	⟨oi⟩, ⟨ou⟩	Review: alphabet order

Read, Write, and Review
- Continue to practice correct letter formation, especially of capital letters and digraphs.
- Regularly review the letter names through reciting/singing the alphabet without prompting.
- Review the lower-case letters and their corresponding capitals, encouraging neat and accurate handwriting (Jolly Phonics Alphabet Poster / flashcards / upper- and lower-case letter matching / capital and word dictation).
- Practice writing words with digraphs, using model sentences.

Reading comprehension for each lesson:

	1	2	3	4	5	6	7	8	9	10	11	12	13
Words and Sentences	out at sea	yes or no	at the park	read and match	read and draw	sentence matching	read, write, and color	in the zoo	having a party	the bad-tempered goat	crossword clues	on the beach	the midnight feast

Words and Sentences
- Use a range of activities to improve the students' blending abilities and develop their reading comprehension skills. Include text that uses the alternative letter-sound spellings and tricky words that have been taught so far, as well as longer and more challenging words.
- Write independently in various ways: on a chosen theme; retelling stories; writing about pictures; describing their own experiences. The students' spelling will not always be accurate, but their work should be readable.

	1	2	3	4	5	6	7	8	9	10	11	12	13
Tricky Words	any, many	more, before	other, were	because, want	saw, put	could, should, would	right, two, four	goes, does	made, their	once, upon, always	also, of, eight	love, cover, after	every, mother, father

Tricky Words
- Encourage the students to read the tricky words and identify the tricky part(s).
- Use various strategies to practice writing the tricky words.
- Use flashcards and dictation to review reading and writing the tricky words that have been taught.
- Write sentences from dictation using regular words and the tricky words already taught.
- From Unit 1, sufficient teaching has been covered to introduce the Jolly Phonics Readers, Green Level, for confident readers who have finished the Yellow Level.

A Brief Overview of the Program

What is Jolly Phonics?

Jolly Phonics is a multisensory program that teaches young students the skills they need to read and write fluently in their first year of school, although the basic principles of the program cover the skills needed for learning to read and write whatever the age. The teaching is divided into three parts or "steps," the timetables for which are shown on the preceding pages. The Jolly Phonics Handbook provides step-by-step lesson plans for Step 1, teacher guidance on lessons for Steps 2 and 3, and reproducible worksheets across the year for the students. This structured approach is suited to whole-school, whole-class teaching but it also works well with individual students.

At the heart of the program is the teaching of the English alphabetic code, which expresses the relationship between the sounds that can be heard in words and the letter(s) that are used to represent those sounds. When students read a word, they are decoding: They look at the letters, recognize the sounds they represent, and blend the sounds to hear the word. When the students write a word, they are encoding: They listen for the sounds in the word and write the letters that represent those sounds. English has a complex written alphabetic code (see the chart on pages 20 and 21), which is why it needs to be systematically and carefully taught. Step 1 of Jolly Phonics teaches the students one way to write each letter sound and Steps 2 and 3 introduce and review the main alternative spellings. Jolly Grammar, which covers spelling, grammar, and punctuation, extends the teaching over the next six years.

The principal aim of Jolly Phonics is to teach students the five key skills that they need to apply the English alphabetic code successfully in their reading and writing. Once the students have mastered these skills, Jolly Phonics continues to extend and consolidate the learning, introducing the students to alternative letter-sound spellings, new tricky words, basic sentence structure, pre-dictionary skills, and reading comprehension. Step 1 teaches the five key skills, while Steps 2 and 3 consolidate and extend the learning.

Jolly Phonics has been developed by classroom teachers and has a tried and tested record of success in many different places and settings around the world. Teachers following this method can be assured that their students will read and write independently much more quickly. Case studies and links to research can be found on the Jolly Learning website.

The five key skills taught in Jolly Phonics

Jolly Phonics Step 1 teaches the five key skills for reading and writing:

1. Learning the letter sounds
2. Learning letter formation
3. Blending (for reading)
4. Identifying the sounds in words (for writing)
5. Tricky words

The first four skills are taught simultaneously. Each lesson introduces a new letter sound and teaches the students how to write the letter(s) that represent the sound. The students then practice blending and segmenting words which use that sound.

The tricky words are taught by saying the word, blending the sounds, and encouraging the students to identify the tricky part of the spelling. As a result, they are not introduced until the sound /sh/ is taught. By then the students have had plenty of blending practice and know most of the letter sounds.

There are 40+ sounds in English, which is considerably more than there are letters in the alphabet. Step 1 introduces them at a rate of one sound a day. Most students are very capable of coping with this fast and stimulating pace. However, the rate of introduction can be adjusted according to the number and duration of lessons available and the age of the students. Audio for the 42 main letter sounds is available from the Resource Bank on the Jolly Learning website, along with many other useful resources for teachers and parents, including videos, activities, and worksheets.

How to use the Jolly Phonics Handbook

For ease of use, the Jolly Phonics Handbook is divided into two distinct sections. The first part introduces the Jolly Phonics program and explains the methodology. It is important to read this before using the worksheets in the classroom. The second part provides reproducible material that can be used with the students. The reproducible sections are divided into the five main skills for Step 1, followed by the weekly topics covered in Steps 2 and 3: Alternative Spellings, Handwriting, and Words and Sentences. (The reproducible material for Tricky Words spans all three steps.) The teaching in Steps 2 and 3 is not intended to take up all the time allocated for English lessons. This means that teachers are free to teach other aspects of literacy, such as comprehension and creative writing, in the remaining time.

Supplementary materials

Jolly Phonics has a wealth of supplementary materials to help teachers deliver the program in a fun and engaging way. These include the Jolly Phonics Cards, Jolly Phonics Word Bank, Finger Phonics Books (two sizes are available for either individual use or whole-class teaching), Jolly Songs, Jolly Phonics Wall Frieze, Tricky Word Wall Flowers, Jolly Phonics Little Word Books, Jolly Phonics Readers, and the Jolly Phonics Alternative Spelling and Alphabet Posters.

Parental support

Learning to read and write fluently is vital for students. All parents know this and want their children to master these skills. The majority of parents are keen to help, but are often not sure how to go about it. It is a good idea to invite new parents to a meeting, where it is explained to them how reading and writing is taught in the school. These meetings provide an opportunity to introduce parents to the five key skills and to explain to them how they can support their children. Explain that any homework that is sent home, such as blending words for reading, will be something their child can already do in the classroom. The aim of homework is to bring fluency to the skills of blending and segmenting. Information for parents is provided in Reproducible Section 1, for copying and handing out.

Assessment

The Jolly Phonics Student Checklist on page 22 provides teachers with an understanding of what the students should learn in the first year. It is also useful for tracking and recording the progress of any individual students who struggle to keep up with the rest of the class. More detailed midterm assessments can be found in the Resource Bank on the Jolly Learning website.

Support for students who struggle to learn the basic skills

In every class there will be a few students who find it difficult to memorize the letter sounds and who struggle to blend and segment words. These students tend to have a weak visual memory and/or poor auditory skills. However, this does not mean that they need different teaching from the other students. In fact, they need the same teaching, but far more of it.

It is important to identify any struggling students in the first few weeks. If possible, it is a good idea to provide some extra teaching for these students. Not all of the students who are struggling will be at the same stage; there will be a range of abilities. Some students will only need extra support for a few weeks before they begin to make steady progress. Other students may have more significant difficulties. Despite their differences, all the students should receive the same type of teaching. With regular blending and writing practice and by reviewing the letter sounds, teachers can ensure that the students master the five skills. For more information on how to support struggling students, see pages 17 to 19.

Teaching the Five Key Skills in Jolly Phonics

1. Learning the letter sounds

It is generally accepted that there are approximately 44 sounds in English; however, only 26 letters are used to represent those sounds and many of them can be spelled in different ways. Two, three, or even four letters are combined to represent the sounds. Initially, the students are introduced to the 42 main sounds and taught one way to represent each of them.

Each letter sound is introduced through a story and an action to help the students remember it. At the same time, the students are shown how the sound is represented in writing. There is a sound sheet for the students to complete, which includes practice for letter formation (Reproducible Section 2).

Once a letter sound has been taught, it can be added to each student's sound book, which is taken home for extra practice (Reproducible Section 4). Reinforcement of the letter sounds is really important both at home and at school. Flashcards should be held up every day in a random order, so that the students can call out the sounds and do the actions (Reproducible Section 3). The faster the students become at recognizing the letters and saying the sounds, the easier it is for them to read and write. Slower learners tend to copy the other students and will need extra practice in small groups.

The letter-sound groups listed below are used in Jolly Phonics:

1. s, a, t, i, p, n
2. c k, e, h, r, m, d
3. g, o, u, l, f, b
4. ai, j, oa, ie, ee, or
5. z, w, ng, v, little oo, long oo
6. y, x, ch, sh, voiced th, unvoiced th
7. qu, ou, oi, ue, er, ar

Jolly Phonics follows the convention of using different symbols to distinguish between letter names and letter sounds: the word *ship* for example, starts with the letter ‹s› and the sound /sh/. Initially, it is important to use the letter sounds when teaching the students how to read and write, not the letter names. If the students try to use the letter names when blending, they will not hear the word. Letter names are only needed when the students start to learn the alphabet, which is introduced in Step 2.

2. Learning letter formation

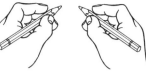

For young students to learn fluent and neat handwriting, they need to be taught how to hold their pencil and how to form letters correctly. It is much better to teach this correctly from the start and early mastery is well worth the effort. Trying to correct bad habits later on is extremely difficult, if not impossible. Regular letter-sound dictation and parental support can be invaluable here.

Step 1 concentrates on the formation of the lower-case letters. Later, in Step 2, the formation of the capital letters is taught, along with alphabet work and a review of common letter shapes (Reproducible Section 12). Capital letters are the same size as tall letters; they all start at or near the top, and they never join.

3. Blending

When reading, students need to understand the meaning of the words, but before they can do this, they have to be able to work out what the words say. In order to do this, the students look at the letters, say the sounds, run them together, and listen for the word. This process is called blending, which is also sometimes referred to as synthesizing. This is why Jolly Phonics is known as a synthetic phonics program.

Once the students can hear the word when an adult says the letter sounds, they are ready to try saying the sounds and listening for the word by themselves. It helps to hear the word if the first sound is stressed and the following sounds are said quickly and softly. The actions should not be used when blending. The blending of regular words needs plenty of practice and should be done every day with the class, as well as in small groups, pairs, or individually, as necessary. When the students become fluent, they should be encouraged to say and blend the sounds silently in their heads, only saying the word aloud. After a word has been blended a few times, it becomes known and then blending is only needed for reading unfamiliar words. The students should never be expected to read words that use letter sounds that have not yet been taught.

There are words for blending on the sound sheets and word banks of suitable words in the lesson plans for Step 1. The students start to use word boxes (Reproducible Section 5) in school or at home once the fifth group of letter sounds has been taught. Once the students are fluent at blending words, they can be given a reading book. Initially, it is important that only decodable books are used. This means books which only use the letter sounds and tricky words that have been taught. Students gain confidence and fluency when they can reliably work out the words for themselves and their letter-sound knowledge is reinforced. The Timetables for Steps 1, 2, and 3 show when the Little Word Books and Jolly Phonics Readers can be introduced.

4. Identifying the sounds in words

In order to write words, the students must be able to say a word, hear the sounds in that word, say the sounds in order, and then write the letters for those sounds. The ability to hear the sounds in words is called phonemic awareness.

From the beginning, the students are taught to hear the sounds in words. The students do not need to have been taught the sounds to do this. The first step is to ask the students to listen for the target sound. For example, in the first lesson, the teacher could ask the students whether there is a /s/ sound in the words *sun, grass,* and *dog*. The next step is to ask the students to listen and identify all the sounds in short words (also known as segmenting).

This skill is modeled by the teacher from the start, using the pictures on the sound sheets, but over time the students should try to do this for themselves. Some students hear the sounds easily and others will require more help. Initially, the students can say the sounds and use magnetic letters or letter cards to spell the word. When the students are confident about identifying the sounds in short words, longer words can be tackled.

Dictation is an excellent way of developing writing. It can begin with calling out letter sounds for the students to write and then move on to words, phrases, and sentences. Regular dictation is provided in the lesson plans for Step 1 and then in the homework writing sheets for Step 2 (Reproducible Section 9). Again, it is important to only ask the students to write words that use the letter sounds they have been taught.

5. Tricky words

Tricky words are so called because they have a tricky part that cannot be worked out simply by blending and listening for the sounds. The tricky part is often simply an alternative spelling that has not been taught yet, but even when it has been taught, the word remains tricky for students to spell unless they have lots of practice writing it. Many of them are frequently used words which need to be known in order to read and write simple sentences.

A total of 72 tricky words is taught in Jolly Phonics, with two or three words usually taught together. The first tricky word, *I,* is introduced in the lesson for /sh/, so that the second word *the* can be taught in the next lesson, alongside the voiced sound /th/. By this stage, the students are able to apply their phonic knowledge to help them work out which part is tricky and this extra attention to detail helps to store the word in the students' memories. There are other techniques that can be used to help learn the tricky words and these are found in Reproducible Section 10. It is important that the tricky words are taught in a systematic way and with plenty of practice.

Teaching Guidance for Steps 1, 2, and 3

Step 1

In Reproducible Section 2 there are daily lesson plans that introduce the students to the 42 main sounds of English, along with a worksheet for each one. Each lesson teaches one sound, or two related sounds, and is structured to give the students a solid grounding in the key skills of Jolly Phonics. Each lesson follows a similar pattern and is based on the following activities.

1. Review the letter sounds taught so far, using **flashcards.** This should be done quite quickly as a whole-class activity. By watching the speed at which the students say the sounds and do the actions, it is easy to identify those who need more help. Shuffle the flashcards beforehand so that the letter sounds come up in a different order each time. This way, related sounds, such as ‹ee› and ‹or› do not follow each other. It is important that the students learn to recognize the sounds when they see them, rather than relying on a set order.

2. Introduce the new letter sound with a story, based on the **storyline** provided. It is better to tell the story in your own way, using plenty of words with the target sound and making it as relevant as possible for the students. Stress the target sound when it appears and encourage the students to listen for it. Using the story picture in the Finger Phonics Big Book, look for things that have that sound in the word.

3. Show the students how to do the **action** for the letter sound. Young students learn particularly quickly when physical activity is involved, and here they are using movement, sight, hearing, and speech to help them remember the letter sound.

4. Introduce the letter(s) that represent the sound. Although the sound sheets have both upper- and lower-case letters, the students are only taught the lower-case **letter formation** at this point. Show the students how to write the letter and encourage them to form it correctly in the air with their finger. Ask one or two students to write it on the board and then call out some other letter sounds for the students to practice.

5. Practice **blending words** that use the new letter sound. This can be done in one of two ways: aurally, by saying the sounds in a word for the students to blend; or by writing words on the board and pointing to the letter(s) as each sound is said. When blending written words, it is important to use words that only contain the letter sounds that have been taught. The word bank for each lesson has plenty of examples.

6. Practice **identifying the sounds** in words (segmenting). The students do not need to have been taught a sound to hear it in a word. Start by calling out the three picture words from the sound sheet. Sound out the words with the students, holding up a finger for each sound. Repeat the activity, using ten short words from the word bank. Encourage the students to sound out the words by themselves as soon as possible.

7. Give the students the **sound sheet** to complete. Encourage them to form the letters correctly and to color as neatly as they can. Both the blending and segmenting activities use dots to show the number of sounds in a word. Encourage the students to point to the dot as they say the sound.

8. Dictate the letter sounds and words suggested in the lesson plan. Ask the students to **listen and write** them down. Afterwards, sound out each word for the students, writing the letters on the board so that they can check their work.

9. From the /sh/ lesson onwards, start introducing the first set of **tricky words**. Together, work out which part of each word is tricky and underline it in purple on the board. If the Tricky Word Wall Flowers are available, this is a good time to put the new word(s) on display. Any new tricky words that have been taught should be reviewed with the letter sounds at the start of the lesson.

10. Finish the lesson by singing the letter-sound song from Jolly Songs and pinning up the relevant section of the Jolly Phonics Wall Frieze. If there is time, use craft activities to help the students learn and remember the letter sounds. Some are suggested in the lesson plans, but there are plenty of **further ideas** in the Jolly Phonics Bumper Book of Phonics Fun.

Step 2

Steps 2 and 3 are divided into 13 weekly units, each with lessons covering four main topics. The topics in Step 2 consolidate and extend the teaching by introducing the main alternative spellings, capital letters, the alphabet, further tricky words, and model sentence writing. These topics can be taught over four days of the week, leaving a day for other areas of literacy learning.

The Jolly Phonics Handbook does not provide lesson plans and worksheets for each lesson in Steps 2 and 3. Instead, teachers can create their own lesson plans, using the scope and sequence mapped out in the timetables and following the guidance in the outline lessons below. A range of worksheets relevant to the topics is provided in Reproducible Sections 11 to 14 to support the teaching. The Jolly Phonics Word Bank is an extremely useful resource for choosing suitable words for the activities.

Daily practice

It is important to review the letter sounds and do some blending and segmenting of words every day. This could be done at the beginning of the lesson or at another time.

Go through the sounds at a rapid pace, using flashcards. It is not necessary to review the letter sounds that the students know well every day. Instead, concentrate on those that have been taught recently, that are not so well known, or that may be difficult to pronounce. Once an alternative spelling has been introduced, its flashcard (Reproducible Section 11) can be added to the pack. Some flashcards – for example ‹y› and ‹ow› – will represent more than one sound, so the students should call out all the sounds they know for that spelling. When reviewing /a/, /e/, /i/, /o/, and /u/, remind the students that these are the short vowel sounds. After Unit 6, remind the students that the sounds /ai/, /ee/, /ie/, /oa/, and /ue/ are the long vowels.

Write some words on the board for blending and segmenting. If an alternative spelling has been introduced the week before, include some words with that spelling. Start by asking the students to say the sounds and blend them to read each word. Then remove or hide the words and call them out for the students to segment. The students respond by saying the sounds and holding up a finger for each one. Go through the words at a rapid pace. Then dictate a few letter sounds and words, either to be written on the board or individually by the students. If the students have been taught more than one spelling for a letter sound, tell them to write all the spellings they know for that sound.

Lesson 1: Alternatives

Before introducing an alternative spelling, it is important to review the target sound, the initial spelling, and any other spellings of that sound that have been taught so far. Then the students can be shown a word using the new alternative. Discuss the new spelling, review the formation of the letter(s), and blend around ten words which have the new alternative spelling in them. Choose some more words with the alternative spelling and segment them with the students. Call out the word, say the sounds, and model how to write the word on the board.

There is a sound sheet for each of the alternative vowel spellings in Reproducible Section 11. Once the students have completed them, they could move on to another activity, such as the following: letter, word, and picture matching (Reproducible Section 11); writing or sorting words which use all the spellings taught for the target sound; writing or copying words, phrases, or sentences which use the new spellings; and drawing pictures to illustrate these words, phrases, and sentences.

Lesson 2: Handwriting

Although the students have been taught how to write the lower-case letters, it is important to give them regular practice. It is a good opportunity to check that the students are forming the letters correctly and have a good pencil hold. The first half of Step 2 focuses on reviewing letters in their letter-sound groups and introducing the capitals for these letters. In the second half of Step 2, the lower-case letters are reviewed again, this time grouped according to their letter shape. At the same time, capital letters are reviewed through the students' alphabet work.

The alphabet can be introduced in the first week. Show the students the Jolly Phonics Alphabet Poster and point out that there are no digraphs. Explain that this is because the alphabet is a way of ordering the single letters, not the sounds. This means that when we say the alphabet, we use the letter names and not the letter sounds. The alphabet can then be said or sung at the start of every Handwriting lesson. By week four, the students can start paying attention to the four color-coded groups on the poster: A–E (red), F–M (yellow), N–S (green), and T–Z (blue). Each of these groups represents roughly a quarter of a dictionary. Knowing which of the quarters a letter belongs to will make it easier for the students to look up words when they start to use a dictionary. The extra attention is well worth the effort.

There are lots of activities that can be done to improve the skills taught in the Handwriting lesson, some of which can be found on the handwriting worksheets in Reproducible Section 12. Other activities include saying the alphabet as quickly as possible; identifying which color group a letter belongs to; saying which letters come before or after a given letter; matching upper- and lower-case letters; and capital letter dictation.

Other activities that help to develop independent writing can be taught in this lesson. Phrases and sentences using the target letters can be traced or copied using different types of pens and pencils. Dictation of letter sounds, words, phrases, and sentences can also be done as part of the lesson, although it is beneficial if this is done regularly throughout the week. Homework writing sheets are provided in Reproducible Section 9.

Lesson 3: Tricky words

The students need lots of practice reading and writing tricky words, so it is important to review them at the start of the lesson. The Jolly Phonics Cards include a set of tricky word flashcards, or the Tricky Word Wall Flowers could be used instead. Alternatively, the lists provided in Reproducible Section 10 could be enlarged and made into flashcards. Go through the tricky words, pointing out the parts that are regular and those that are tricky.

The timetables for Steps 2 and 3 show when to introduce each of the new tricky words. For reading, it helps to say the word, blend the sounds in the word with the students, and work out the tricky part together. The students will find it easier to remember the tricky part of the spelling if certain techniques are used, such as "saying it as it sounds" or by pointing out a common spelling pattern (such as those found in *you* and *your* or *go, no,* and *so*). For spelling, the students need lots of practice writing the tricky word. Before they do, they look at the word and find the tricky part. Next, they copy the word, reminding themselves of which parts are regular and which parts are tricky. Then they cover the word and try to write it for themselves, before checking it and writing the word again. Once they have practiced writing the new tricky words several times, the students are ready to try writing the words from dictation.

Again, there are activities that can be done to reinforce the learning of the tricky words, some of which are provided in Reproducible Section 10. Other activities include giving the students some sentences to read that use the new tricky words. The students could then copy the sentence, underlining the tricky parts in purple, and draw a picture to illustrate the sentence. The Jolly Phonics Word Bank includes sentences with tricky words.

Lesson 4: Words and sentences

Now that the students have had plenty of practice segmenting and writing short regular words, it is time to develop their ability to write fluently in sentences, and to build their confidence in tackling any words they wish to write. The lessons in Step 2 do this by providing a writing topic, a picture, and a model sentence to get them started (Reproducible Section 13). At the beginning, the students need plenty of help and guidance.

Use the picture to initiate discussion and to go over vocabulary. Model how to write key words that the students may use, especially words with double letters, schwas, or that use ‹ck› or ‹k›. Write the model sentence on the board, and discuss the following points as you do so:

- All sentences start with a capital letter.
- All capital letters are tall.
- Listen for the sounds in a word to write it.
- Leave a space between words.
- All sentences end with a period.

If there are any tricky words in the model sentence, ask the students how the tricky part should be spelled. Once the sentence is finished, remind the students that they should always read back what they have written and check that it makes sense.

The picture can then be pasted in a book or onto a sheet of paper. The students copy the sentence underneath and color in the picture. Those students who are ready to try writing independently can write some more sentences of their own. At this stage the students are not expected to remember the alternative spellings for writing. Therefore, some of the spelling will not be accurate, but it can be read. As the students' knowledge increases and they read more widely, their spelling will improve.

Other areas of literacy learning

The timetable deliberately sets aside one day for other areas of literacy learning. Teachers are free to choose whatever is best suited to the class, but one suggestion would be to focus on developing the students' comprehension by reading stories and talking about them. The story could be related to a topic being studied, the new alternative spelling for the week, or to a current festival or time of year. Ask the students questions about any unusual words used in the story and about the characters and what happens to them. When the students respond, ask them to think about what information given in the story led them to that answer. This can be followed by an activity connected to the story: for example, acting it out or retelling the story; using sequence pictures or sentences; writing about a favorite character; or drawing a picture.

Step 3

Like Step 2, Step 3 is divided into 13 weekly units, each with lessons covering four main topics. Handwriting is still a focus, but the topic is now called Read, Write, and Review. This is because the focus has shifted away from teaching new content to reviewing and consolidating what has been taught. The other topics in Step 3 consolidate and extend the learning, regularly practicing the alternative spellings and tricky words taught in Step 2, while introducing the remaining tricky words and some new alternative spellings: ‹ph› as /f/, soft ‹c›, soft ‹g›, ‹air›, ‹ear›, and ‹are› for /air/, and ‹ue›, ‹u_e›, and ‹ew› for long /oo/. In Words and Sentences, there is a strong focus on improving the students' reading comprehension skills. These topics can be taught over four days of the week, leaving a day for other areas of literacy learning.

As with Step 2, teachers create their own lesson plans, using the scope and sequence mapped out in the timetable and following the guidance in the outline lessons below. A range of worksheets relevant to the topics is provided in Reproducible Sections 11 to 14 to support the teaching. The Jolly Phonics Word Bank is an extremely useful resource for choosing suitable words for the activities.

Daily practice

This should be similar to Step 2 (see page 13). The focus now is on reviewing the alternative spellings that have been taught (using flashcards) and blending and segmenting words which use those alternative spellings. When new spellings are introduced, they should also be incorporated into the flashcards and blending and segmenting words. Dictate a few letter sounds and words, either to be written on the board or individually by the students. Remind the students to write all the spellings they know for that sound.

Lesson 1: Alternatives

The lessons in Step 3 follow a similar pattern to those in Step 2 (see page 13). The focus now is to introduce the remaining alternative spellings and to review the alternative spellings of the vowel sounds. Some of the blending words for the new alternative spellings are quite challenging, so help the students where necessary. The saying "If the short vowel sound does not work, try the long vowel" is particularly helpful here.

Many spelling rules are associated with the short and long vowels, so it is a good idea to reinforce the students' understanding of them. One way to do this is to use the "vowel hand." Ask the students to hold up their hand. Say the short vowels – /a/, /e/, /i/, /o/, and /u/ – while the students point to the tip of their thumb for /a/, the tip of their index finger for /e/, and so on. Then call out the long vowel sounds – /ai/, /ee/, /ie/, /oa/, and /ue/. This time the students point to the base of their thumb and fingers to indicate the sounds. At this point, the students are only expected to know the alternative spellings for reading and are not expected to use them consistently in their writing. However, by gently introducing some of the basic rules for spelling – such as shy ‹i› and toughy ‹y› or using ‹ck› after a short vowel – and regularly reviewing them in the lessons, the students will start to remember them.

Lesson 2: Read, write, and review

Reviewing letter formation, particularly for the digraphs and capital letters, and consolidating the students' knowledge of the alphabet is the main focus of this lesson in Step 3. Students should continue to recite or sing the alphabet regularly and to work on understanding which letters fall into which color-coded group. Care should be taken to ensure that the students are forming the letters correctly and have a good pencil hold. After Unit 6, practice how to read and write sentences that use the target digraphs in each lesson. Continue to give the students activities similar to those outlined in Step 2 to consolidate the learning (see Handwriting, page 14).

Lesson 3: Tricky words

The lessons in Step 3 follow a similar pattern to those in Step 2 (see page 14) and the timetable shows when to introduce each of the new tricky words. Now that the students have been taught more than half of the tricky words, it is even more important to review them regularly and to use them in sentences for reading and writing. Continue to point out the tricky words that share common spelling patterns, such as *any* and *many* or *should, would,* and *could,* and to use the Look, Cover, Copy, Write, Check method to practice writing the tricky words.

Again, there are activities that can be done to reinforce the learning of the tricky words, some of which are provided in Reproducible Section 10. Other activities include asking the students to fill in the missing letters in the target tricky words, or filling in the missing target words in sentences. The students are also ready to write sentences that use the target tricky words from dictation. The Jolly Phonics Word Bank includes sentences with tricky words.

Lesson 4: Words and sentences

In Step 3, the lessons cover a range of activities (Reproducible Section 14), all of which aim to improve the students' blending abilities and their reading comprehension skills. The text the students have to read in the activities uses the alternative letter-sound spellings and tricky words that have been taught so far. Toward the end of Step 3, more challenging words are sometimes used and these will need to be blended with the students. These words may include the schwa sound, vowel letters saying the long vowel sound, silent letters (shown in light type), or spellings that need a little adjustment to hear the word correctly, such as *water* and *year.* With a little guidance, most students are able to blend these words, especially if the word is in their vocabulary.

If there is time at the end of the lesson, the students should be given the opportunity to do some writing of their own. An extension activity could be suggested, either one linked to the lesson topic, or one of the teacher's own choosing: for example, writing the students' own news, retelling a story, or describing a picture. The students will need plenty of help and guidance to get them started, so it is important to begin with a class discussion about the topic and to write a few of the more challenging key words on the board to help with the spelling. Then the students write as much as they can. The spelling will not always be accurate, but their work will be readable. The students finish by illustrating their work, which could then be collated into a class book.

Other areas of literacy learning

The timetable deliberately sets aside one day for other areas of literacy learning. If there is not time for independent writing in the Words and Sentences lesson, it could be taught here. For some students, thinking up a story and then writing it down is very difficult, as they are concentrating on how to form letters, sounding out individual words, and writing sentences. Once the students are more fluent in their writing, they will find it easier to write their own creative stories, so the extra effort to promote fluency in writing is well worth it.

Support for Students who Struggle to Learn the Basic Skills

Activities for intervention support

The following ideas are merely suggestions. Teachers and teaching assistants will have further ideas of their own. The important thing is to choose activities that focus on practicing the skills that the students most need to improve. It is always important to keep in mind the aim of the intervention session: to catch up and keep up with the rest of the class by learning the letter sounds, blending, segmenting, learning tricky words, and improving spelling.

More information on letter-sound boxes and word-blending boxes can be found in the Resource Bank on the Jolly Learning website or in Preventing Reading and Writing Problems, Parts 1 and 4 at www.tcrw.co.uk. There is further information on the same website for learning the letter sounds (Part 3) and auditory blending (Part 4).

1. Learning the letter sounds

A poor ability to remember the letter sounds is often one of the first indications that difficulties are developing for a student. It is a sign of a weak visual and/or auditory memory. Early intervention is needed in order to develop fluency and automatic recall, as well as to establish the letter sounds in the student's long-term memory.

Intervention can be done one-to-one or as a group. Ideally, when organizing an intervention group, select students of similar learning difficulties and aim to concentrate the teaching on two or more letter-sound correspondences that are not known well enough. It helps to keep in mind the "catch up and keep up" aim when preparing for each session.

Once the students who are having difficulty learning the letter sounds have been identified, they can be given their own letter-sound box. Identify the letter sounds that each student knows reasonably well and place them in his or her box for practice at home or at school. Ideally, someone should listen to the student saying these letter sounds every day. Then, as soon as possible after some intervention support, remove any really well known letter sounds and add others that need extra practice.

Small group activities for learning the letter sounds

Letter-sound activities using flashcards can be done by the teacher or teaching assistant with a group of three or four students, sitting at a table. The simplest activity is to hold up the letter-sound cards, one by one. The students call out the sounds as quickly as possibly as the letters are shown. This can be turned into a race by seeing who can say the sound first. This not only adds a sense of fun but encourages greater fluency and works well with evenly matched students. Whoever says the sound first gets the card; if two students say the sound at the same time, it goes back in the pile. The student with the most cards at the end of the game is the winner.

Another activity involves laying out a few letter-sound cards on the table. One by one, call out the letter sounds and ask a different student to touch the correct card each time. Alternatively, call out each sound and see who is the first to touch the correct card. This is good competitive fun as long as it does not disturb the rest of the students or other classes. Another alternative is to deal out a few cards to each student and ask them to point to the letters and say the sounds as fast as possible. From this you can see which students know their letter sounds and how well they know them.

2. Letter formation

It is important that struggling students learn to form the letters for the sounds correctly and neatly. Writing a few from dictation in each intervention session not only gives an opportunity for checking these skills, it is also an excellent way of reviewing the letter sounds.

It is also important to focus on two particular letter sounds that need extra practice. Show the letter-sound cards to the students and ask if anyone remembers them. Then practice the formation in two stages: firstly, while the students can see the letter sound and then from dictation. The students either write the letter or form it on the table with their finger. Watch carefully to see whether the students form the letters correctly.

3. Blending

Students who struggle to hear a word after they have said the sounds need more auditory blending practice, where the teacher says the sounds and the student listens for the word. Some teachers tap their arm to model auditory blending of CVC words: on the shoulder for the first sound, then on the elbow, and then on the wrist. Then, as they blend the sounds together and say the word, they run their hand down their arm. It is also good to model the blending process with a few words in each session, using the *I say it*, *we say it* and *you say it* approach. This prepares the students for the ultimate skill of blending unknown words.

The simplest auditory blending activity is to say, for example, *I hear, with my little ear, a word. What is it? /f-o-x/*. The students respond, giving the answer *fox*. Alternatively, picture cards or a bag of objects can be used to help the students hear a word when the sounds are said. For example, show two pictures of a cow and a car and ask *Which one is the /c-ar/*? Repeat with other cards and, as the students improve, increase the number of pictures to three or four to make the activity that little bit harder. Another activity involves holding a picture card so that it cannot be seen and saying, for example, *In my hand is a /m-oo-n/. What do I have in my hand?* Whoever says *moon* gets the picture. This can be varied by putting several objects in a bag, such as a book, fork, and comb, and sounding out the object you are holding. As always, it is better to stick to short words.

There are many activities suitable for students who need extra support in improving their blending fluency, including word-blending boxes, targeted practice of initial consonant blends, and targeted practice of blending a consonant and a short vowel. In these sessions it is important to include words that focus on two particular letter sounds that need extra practice.

4. Segmenting

Students who struggle to hear the sounds in words benefit from extra practice. They listen to a word as it is called out and then, with support, say the sounds, holding up a finger for each one. Alternatively, they could tap the back of their hand or tap their head. Hearing the sounds in a word with a consonant blend is more difficult, so encourage the students to say the word slowly: for example, */sss-lll-u-g/*. The students could then make the words using plastic letters or letter-sound cards. Make sure that two letter sounds that need extra practice are used in some of them. Not only do these activities develop the students' ability to hear the sounds in words, they also show the students why they need to be able to do so: namely, to work words out in preparation for writing.

Dictation is the best way to develop the skill of writing. Make sure the dictation includes the two target letter sounds, as well as some words that use those letter sounds. Keep it snappy, ensuring a fast pace.

5. Tricky words

If the whole class is learning the tricky words, start with the first two: *I* and *the*. Teach these words using flashcards and dictation. In addition, use suitable methods to help the students remember how to spell the tricky parts (see page 150).

If there is time, encourage the students to read a few short sentences: for example, *I am hot, The dog is black, The dress has a bad stain.* The sentences should use regular words that can be worked out, as well as the target tricky words. The Jolly Phonics Word Bank is a useful resource for making up sentences. Having blended the words in the sentence once, encourage the students to read them again, this time without the blending.

English Alphabetic Code Chart

The chart below aims to give an overall understanding of the English alphabetic code. The list is not exhaustive and some letter-sound correspondences have hardly any words that use them. Nevertheless it is helpful to see how the code works.

Care should be taken with ‹qu› and ‹x› because technically they each have two sounds blended together: ‹qu› is /kw/ and ‹x› is /ks/. Initially, it is easier for young students to think of them as one sound. Also, it is not necessary to teach the /ier/ sound early on. Young students can blend words like *beer, fear*, and *here* as /b-ee-r/, /f-ea-r/, and /h-ee-r/ and hear the word, without needing to know that technically each has an /ier/ sound.

/s/	/a/	/t/	/i/	/p/	/n/
sun fuss cent cinema cycle bounce house castle psalm answer science	ant	ten mitten hopped debt waste cassette thyme pterodactyl two	ink pyramid biscuit minute sausage women bargain seive	pet happy shepherd	net funny know gnat gone pneumonia mnemonic

/c k/	/e/	/h/	/r/	/m/	/d/
cat kitten duck chemist conquer unique occur Iraq khaki	egg head heifer leopard said says friend any bury	hat who	rat carrot write rhino	man hammer lamb hymn come	dog teddy cleaned jodhpurs

/g/	/o/	/u/	/l/	/f/	/b/
gap foggy ghost guide vague	odd was haul talk saw cough bought caught knowledge	under love country blood does	leg bell gazelle	fun off photo tough giraffe	bat rabbit

/ai/	/j/	/oa/	/ie/	/ee/	/or/
aim lake play vein weigh they apron ballet great sundae straight	jam gentle giant gym large adjust bridge	oak hope slow go toe dough plateau soul sew oh mauve	pie time night sky find eider aisle bye buy height eye ayah	bee sunny theme dream chief key we receive radio larvae people	order shore warm soar four door dinosaur

/z/	/w/	/ng/	/v/	/oo/	/oo/
zoo buzz is rouse snooze scissors Wednesday xylophone	web whistle penguin	sing wink	van sleeve of savvy	book push could woman	moon blue rude drew flu do fruit soup through sleuth shoe oeuvre lieu

/y/	/x/	/ch/	/sh/	/th/	/th/
yes onion	fox hooks lakes ducks excellent accept	chop hatch nature	ship machine musician station tension tissue sugar crèche appreciate permission fashion schwa	this soothe	thin

/qu/	/ou/	/oi/	/ue/	/er/	/ar/
queen	out owl bough	oil boy buoy	rescue cube few unicorn feud beautiful	herb bird hurt learn word were grammar pressure zephyr purr chauffeur	arm heart sergeant are

/air/	/zh/	/ool/	/ier/	schwa /uh/	
chair stare pear where aerobic their prayer parent	vision treasure courgette seizur collage	apple local label pencil cymbol tearful	fierce near cheer hero	the extra possibly today	minus anxious martyr Michael

Jolly Phonics: Student Checklist

Name: .... Date: ....

	Says sound in response to letter(s)	Writes letter(s) in response to sound	Blends regular words with these sounds	Writes regular words with these sounds
s a t i p n				
ck e h r m d				
g o u l f b				
ai j oa ie ee or				
z w ng v oo oo				
y x ch sh th th				
qu ou oi ue er ar				
y¹ a_e e_e i_e o_e u_e				
ay oy ea y igh ow²				
ir ur ew aw au al				

¹‹y› as /ee/   ²‹ow› as /oa/ and /ou/

	Says sound in response to letter(s)	Writes letter(s) in response to sound	Blends regular words with these sounds	Writes regular words with these sounds
ph soft c soft g ue³ u_e³ ew³				
air ear are				

³‹ue›, ‹u_e›, ‹ew› as long /oo/

	Knows letter sound	Knows letter name	Forms letter correctly
Alphabet: lower-case letters			
Alphabet: capital letters			

	Can sing/recite	Knows the 4 alphabet quarters
Alphabet order		

	1-12	13-24	25-36	37-48	49-60	61-72
Able to read tricky words						
Able to write tricky words						

	Slowly	Steadily	Fluently
Able to read regular words, phrases, and sentences			

	With consonant blends	With digraphs	In phrases	In sentences using known tricky words
Able to write from dictation regular words				

Information for Parents

1. Learning the letter sounds

In Jolly Phonics, the main sounds of English are taught, not just the alphabet sounds. For each sound there is an action, which helps the students remember the sound the letter makes. As the letter sounds are taught, they are pasted into a sound book that will be brought home. If possible, go through the sound book with your child every day.

The letter sounds are not introduced in alphabetical order. The ones in the first groupn– /s, a, t, i, p, n/ – have been chosen because they make more simple words than any other six letters. Some sounds can be written in more than one way, but the students are taught only one at the beginning; for instance, the sound /ai/, as in *rain*, is taught initially, while the alternatives, ‹a_e› (as in *cake*) and ‹ay› (as in *day*), will be taught later. All the sounds can be heard on the Jolly Learning website, in the audio and video section of the Resource Bank.

2. Letter formation

It is very important that your child holds a pencil correctly. The pencil rests between the thumb and the first finger; the next finger prevents the pencil falling down, and the last two fingers are tucked away. This pencil hold applies equally to both left- and right-handed children. If the hold is wrong, it is very difficult to correct later on. The correct formation for each letter can be seen on the bottom of each sound sheet.

3. Blending

Blending is the process of saying the sounds in a word and then running them together to make the word: /c-a-t/ is *cat*, for example. It is a technique your child will need to learn and it improves with practice, although this takes longer for some students than others. To start with, you should say the individual sounds in a word and see if your child can hear it. The sounds must be said quickly to hear the word, and it is easier if the first sound is said slightly louder, as in /**b**-u-s/. Initially, some support will be needed, and you may have to run the sounds together and almost say the word before your child will hear it.

After about six weeks, when your child knows many of the letters sounds and has started blending words in school, (s)he will start to bring home word boxes. Please listen as your child blends the sounds and reads the words, and then return the box to school. Once your child has been through the word boxes and is confidently blending words, (s)he will be given a decodable reading book to bring home. Please listen to your child read as often as possible.

4. Identifying sounds in words

To write independently, your child needs to be able to hear the sounds in words and to write the letters for those sounds. When your child is able to hear the sounds in words, a homework writing book will be sent home, along with a list of words. One by one, call out each word. Your child has to listen for the sounds and write down the letters to make the word. This is the first step toward independent writing. Once your child can write words confidently, phrases and sentences will be sent home. As well as writing the individual words, your child will have to remember the rest of the phrase or sentence. The sentences may include one or more tricky words: *I, the, he, she, me, we, be, was, to, do, are,* or *all.* Remind your child to think about how these are spelled and to leave spaces between all the words.

5. Tricky words

Some common words that are needed to write sentences are not entirely regular. You cannot simply blend the sounds together to read the word or listen for the sounds and write the letters to get the correct spelling. This is either because the spelling is irregular or, more commonly, because the word has a letter-sound spelling that has not been taught yet. These parts of the word are "tricky" and have to be learned. As your child becomes more fluent at reading and writing, (s)he will be taught how to cope with tricky words.

Finally

This all sounds like a great deal of work, but it goes in stages and is spread over a considerable period of time. Where practice is concerned, little and often is best and your child may sometimes be tired after school. If so, it is better not to push too hard and to leave any homework for another day. Any parental help and support is a bonus at this young age, and it is much appreciated by the students, as well as the teacher.

Further help, advice, and resources can be found in the Resource Bank on the Jolly Learning website at **www.jollylearning.com**. This includes audio of the letter sounds, a list of the actions, and a complex alphabetic code chart.

Lesson Plans and Sound Sheets

There are 40 or more sounds in English. In Jolly Phonics, 42 letter sounds are taught, together with the letters that relate to those sounds. The initial focus is on teaching the letter sounds and the skills needed to blend and segment words for reading and writing. By not introducing decodable reading books until this learning is secure, most students can learn the sounds in eight weeks. The letters are introduced in an interesting way, involving plenty of action and fun. Parents can contribute by playing letter sound activities and word games with their children and by regularly going through their child's sound book.

For each of the letter sounds there is a suggested storyline, an action, and a sound sheet. The suggested storyline is deliberately brief to encourage teachers to tell the story in their own way, making it as relevant as possible for the students. The sound sheet has a picture for the students to color in that relates to the story, as well as a line with some dotted letters. The students use this to practice writing the letter(s) for the sound, first by going over the dots and then by trying on their own. On the left-hand side of the sheet there are some words for blending. These words only use the letter sounds that have been taught so far, so the students should be able to blend them together to hear the word. Once a sound sheet has been completed, the students can take it home and show their parents, who will see the progress being made.

In Jolly Phonics, the 42 letter sounds are organized in seven groups of six sounds. They are intended to be taught in order, starting with /s/ in group 1 and ending with /ar/ in group 7. The majority of students are able to learn five new letter sounds a week. The sound sheets on the following pages are presented in the recommended teaching order:

1. s, a, t, i, p, n

2. c k, e, h, r, m, d

3. g, o, u, l, f, b

4. ai, j, oa, ie, ee, or

5. z, w, ng, v, little oo, long oo

6. y, x, ch, sh, voiced th, unvoiced th

7. qu, ou, oi, ue, er, ar

Letter Sound: /s/

Storyline: It is a sunny day and a boy is taking his dog for a walk. The boy throws a stick and the dog chases after it. The dog sniffs around in the grass and starts barking. A large, spotty snake is sitting up and hissing: "Sssss!" The boy grabs the dog and the snake slowly slithers away.

 Action: The students weave their hand like a snake, while making a continuous /ssssss/ sound.

Letter formation: Explain how the letter for /s/ is written. The students form the letter in the air. Then they practice writing the letter on their sound sheets. They write over the dotted letters and then try again, using the starting dots.

Blending: Look at the sound sheet and say the sound /s/ with the students. Encourage them to point to the dot under the sound as they say it. Then do some auditory blending. Call out the sounds in a word and ask the students to blend them together and say the word. For example, say the sounds in *sun* – /s-u-n/ – and encourage the students to call out "sun."

Identifying the sounds: This activity is for aural segmenting only. Look at the three small pictures on the sound sheet. Say the words and then sound them out with the students, holding up a finger for each sound: s-u-n, s-o-ck, s-n-ai-l. Say the sounds again, pointing to the dots under the words.

Sound sheet: Encourage the students to form the letters correctly and to color the pictures neatly when completing the sound sheet.

Further ideas
• Sing the /s/ song from Jolly Songs.
• Make snake shapes from dough or modeling clay.
• Paint ‹s› snakes cut out of paper or card and make mobiles or a collage.
• Pin up the /s/ section of the Wall Frieze.

Letter Sound: /a/

Flashcards: Review the letter sound /s/.

Storyline: A family is having a picnic. Dad has packed some apples, plenty of jam sandwiches, cans of orange juice, and a blackberry pie. Suddenly, the children feel something tickling them on their arm. There are ants everywhere! Everyone jumps up from the picnic blanket, shouting, "a, a, a, a!"

 **Action:** The students pretend that ants are crawling up their arm and say *a, a, a, a*.

Letter formation: Explain how the letter for /a/ is written. The students form the letter in the air. Then they practice writing the letter on their sound sheets. They write over the dotted letters and then try again, using the starting dots.

Blending: Look at the sound sheet and say the sounds /s/ and /a/ with the students. Encourage them to point to the dot under each sound as they say it. Then do some auditory blending. Call out the sounds in a word and ask the students to blend them together and say the word. For example, say the sounds in *ant* – /a-n-t/ – and encourage the students to call out "ant."

Identifying the sounds: This activity is for aural segmenting only. Look at the three small pictures on the sound sheet. Say the words and then sound them out with the students, holding up a finger for each sound: a-n-t, h-a-t, a-rr-ow. Say the sounds again, pointing to the dots under the words.

Sound sheet: Encourage the students to form the letters correctly and to color the pictures neatly when completing the sound sheet.

Listen and write: Call out the sounds /a/ and /s/ and ask the students to write the letter for each one.

Further ideas
• Sing the /a/ song from Jolly Songs.
• Cut some apples in half and use them to print colorful shapes.
• Paint large letter ‹a›s cut out of paper or card and make mobiles or a collage.
• Pin up the /a/ section of the Wall Frieze.

A a

s ⋮ a ⋮

Letter Sound: /t/

Flashcards: Review the letter sounds already taught: /s/, /a/.

Storyline: Two children go to a tennis match. It is very exciting. Each time the racket hits the ball, it makes a /t/ noise. The people in the crowd turn their heads from side to side, watching the ball. When the children go home, they play tennis too, taking it in turns to hit the ball: "t, t, t, t."

 **Action:** The students pretend to watch a game of tennis, turning their heads from side to side as they say *t, t, t, t.*

Letter formation: Explain how the letter for /t/ is written, pointing out that it is a tall letter and starts slightly higher than the letters ‹s› and ‹a›. The students form the letter in the air. Then they practice writing the letter on their sound sheets. They write over the dotted letters and then try again, using the starting dots.

Blending: Blend the words on the sound sheet with the students: *at, sat.* The students point to the dot underneath each sound as they say it.

Identifying the sounds: This activity is for aural segmenting only. Look at the three small pictures on the sound sheet. Say the words and then sound them out with the students, holding up a finger for each sound: t-r-ee, t-e-dd-y, t-e-n-t. Say the sounds again, pointing to the dots under the words.

Sound sheet: Encourage the students to form the letters correctly and to color the pictures neatly when completing the sound sheet.

Listen and write: Call out the sounds /t/, /a/, /s/ and ask the students to write the letter for each one.

Further ideas
• Sing the /t/ song from Jolly Songs.
• Make model turtles from modeling clay.
• Ask the students to bring in their teddies and have a teddy bear day.
• Pin up the /t/ section of the Wall Frieze.

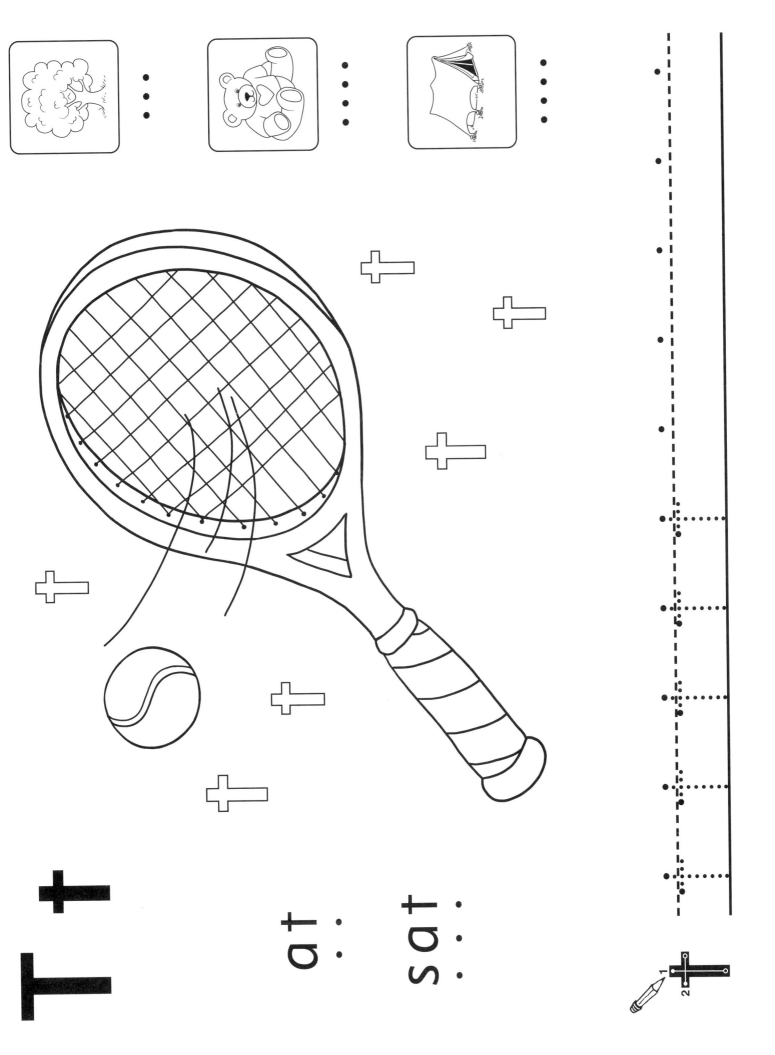

Letter Sound: /i/

Flashcards: Review the letter sounds already taught: /s/, /a/, /t/.

Storyline: One night, a white pet mouse escapes from her cage. She runs along the desk, knocking over a bottle of ink. The lid comes off and the ink spills everywhere, splashing the little mouse; "i, i, i, i," she squeaks as she scrubs her fur, but the ink will not come off. Now she is known as Inky Mouse.

 Action: The students pretend to be a mouse stroking its whiskers and say *i, i, i, i.*

Letter formation: Explain how the letter for /i/ is written. The students form the letter in the air. Then they practice writing the letter on their sound sheets. They write over the dotted letters and then try again, using the starting dots.

Blending: Blend the words on the sound sheet with the students: *it, sit.* The students point to the dot underneath each sound as they say it.

Identifying the sounds: This activity is for aural segmenting only. Look at the three small pictures on the sound sheet. Say the words and then sound them out with the students, holding up a finger for each sound: h-i-ll, i-n(g)-k, i-g-l-oo. Say the sounds again, pointing to the dots under the words.

Sound sheet: Encourage the students to form the letters correctly and to color the pictures neatly when completing the sound sheet.

Listen and write: Call out the sounds /i/, /t/, /a/, /s/ and ask the students to write the letter for each one.

Further ideas
• Sing the /i/ song from Jolly Songs.
• Make pictures from inky fingerprints.
• Hunt around the classroom, looking for the letter ‹i› in books and on posters.
• Pin up the /i/ section of the Wall Frieze.

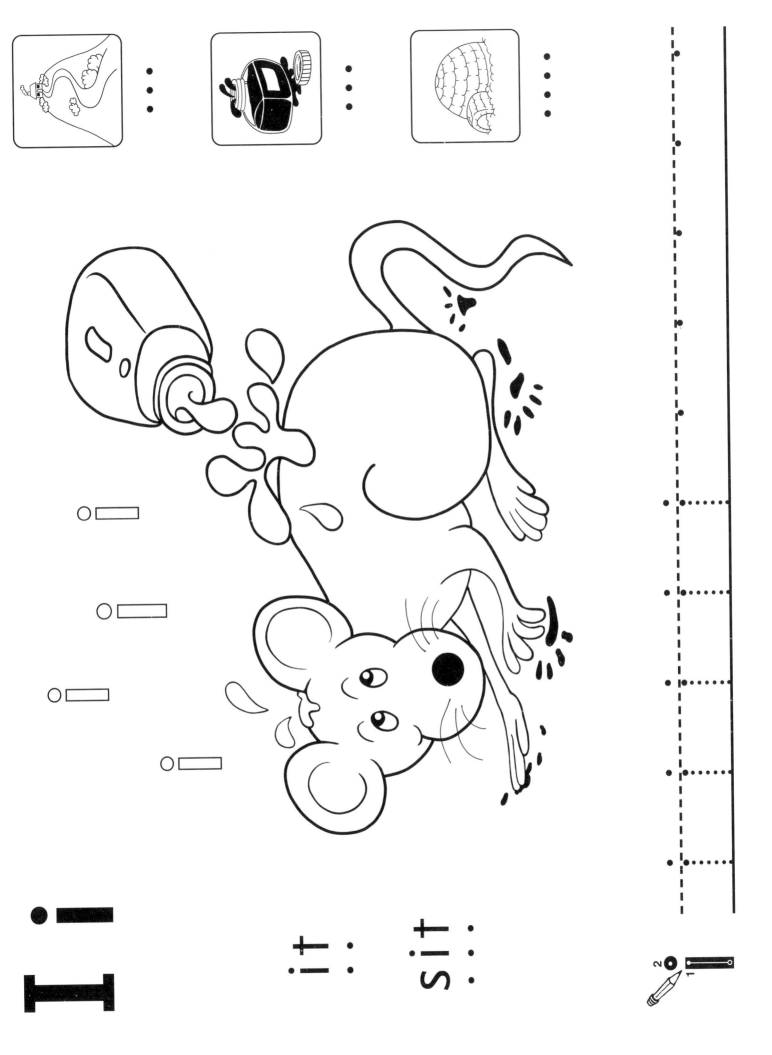

I i

.it :

sit :

Letter Sound: /p/

Flashcards: Review the letter sounds already taught: /s/, /a/, /t/, /i/.

Storyline: Bee is having a birthday party with her friends. She opens her presents and plays some party games. Then she tries to puff out the candles on her big pink cake, but every time she blows one out, it lights up again. They are trick candles! Everyone laughs and tries to puff out the candles: "p, p, p, p."

 Action: The students hold up their finger as if it is a candle and pretend to puff it out saying *p, p, p, p*.

Letter formation: Explain how the letter for /p/ is written, pointing out that it has a tail that goes down under the line. The students form the letter in the air. Then they practice writing the letter on their sound sheets. They write over the dotted letters and then try again, using the starting dots.

Blending: Blend the words on the sound sheet with the students: *pit, pat, tip, tap.* The students point to the dot underneath each sound as they say it. More words from the word bank can be written on the board for extra blending practice.

Identifying the sounds: This activity is for aural segmenting only. Look at the three small pictures on the sound sheet. Say the words and then sound them out with the students, holding up a finger for each sound: p-ie, p-a-n, p-o-n-d. Say the sounds again, pointing to the dots under the words. Do some more segmenting, using short words from the word bank.

Word bank: pat, pip, pit, sap, sip, tap, tip, spat, spit.

Sound sheet: Encourage the students to form the letters correctly and to color the pictures neatly when completing the sound sheet.

Listen and write: Call out the sounds /p/, /i/, /t/, /a/, /s/ and ask the students to write the letter for each one.

Further ideas
• Sing the /p/ song from Jolly Songs.
• Make a collage of parrots with feathers.
• Paint pictures of porcupines or pink poodles.
• Pin up the /p/ section of the Wall Frieze.

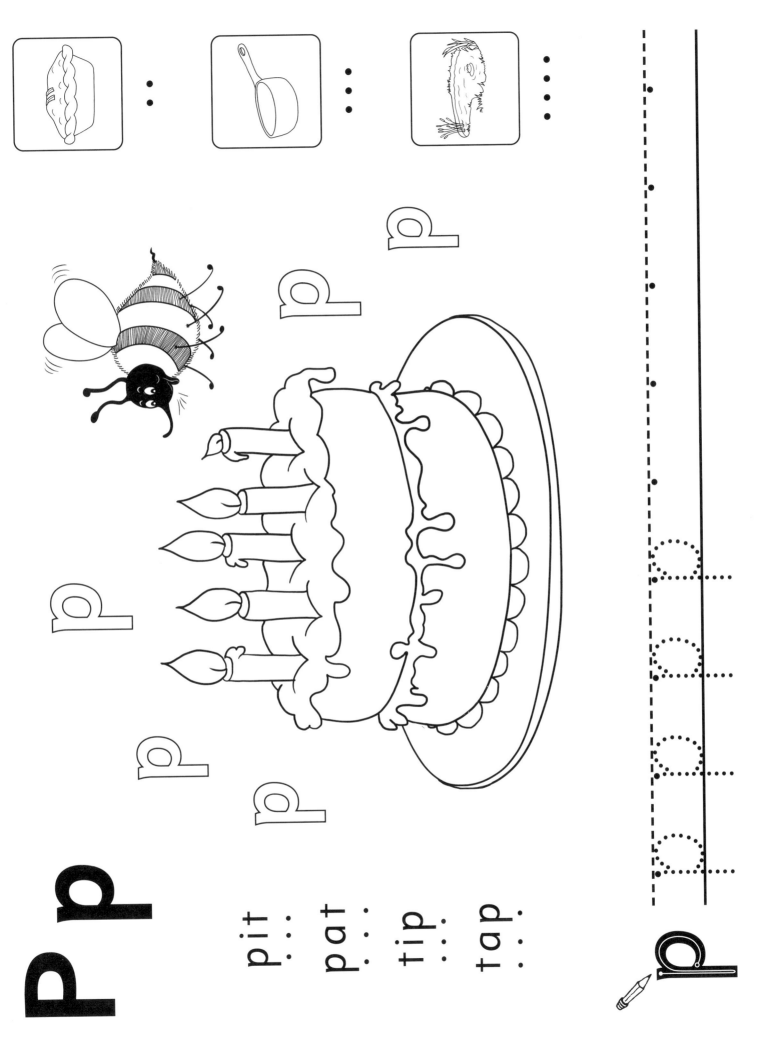

P p

p p
p p

pit
pat
tip
tap

p

Letter Sound: /n/

Flashcards: Review the letter sounds already taught: /s/, /a/, /t/, /i/, /p/.

Storyline: Inky and Snake are having fun, flying a plane. They do a noisy loop-the-loop and fly low over a pond. A girl and her grandfather are fishing with a net and the plane makes them jump. "What a nasty noise," the grandfather says, but the little girl laughs. She holds out her arms and pretends to fly like a plane: "nnnnnn!"

 Action: The students put their arms out and pretend to be a nasty noisy plane, making a continuous /nnnnnn/ sound.

Letter formation: Explain how the letter for /n/ is written. The students form the letter in the air. Then they practice writing the letter on their sound sheets. They write over the dotted letters and then try again, using the starting dots.

Blending: Blend the words on the sound sheet with the students: *tin, ant, nip, pan.* The students point to the dot underneath each sound as they say it. More words from the word bank can be written on the board for extra blending practice.

Identifying the sounds: This activity is for aural segmenting only. Look at the three small pictures on the sound sheet. Say the words and then sound them out with the students, holding up a finger for each sound: n-e-t, n-u-t, n-e-s-t. Say the sounds again, pointing to the dots under the words. Do some more segmenting, using short words from the word bank.

Word bank: an, in, ant, nap, nip, nit, pan, pin, tan, tin, pant, snap, snip, span, spin, tint, insist; a pin.

Sound sheet: Encourage the students to form the letters correctly and to color the pictures neatly when completing the sound sheet.

Listen and write: Call out the sounds /n/, /p/, /i/, /t/, /a/, /s/ and ask the students to write the letter for each one.

Further ideas
• Sing the /n/ song from Jolly Songs.
• Think of some nasty noisy things and draw pictures of them.
• Make nests from twigs and moss.
• Pin up the /n/ section of the Wall Frieze.

N n

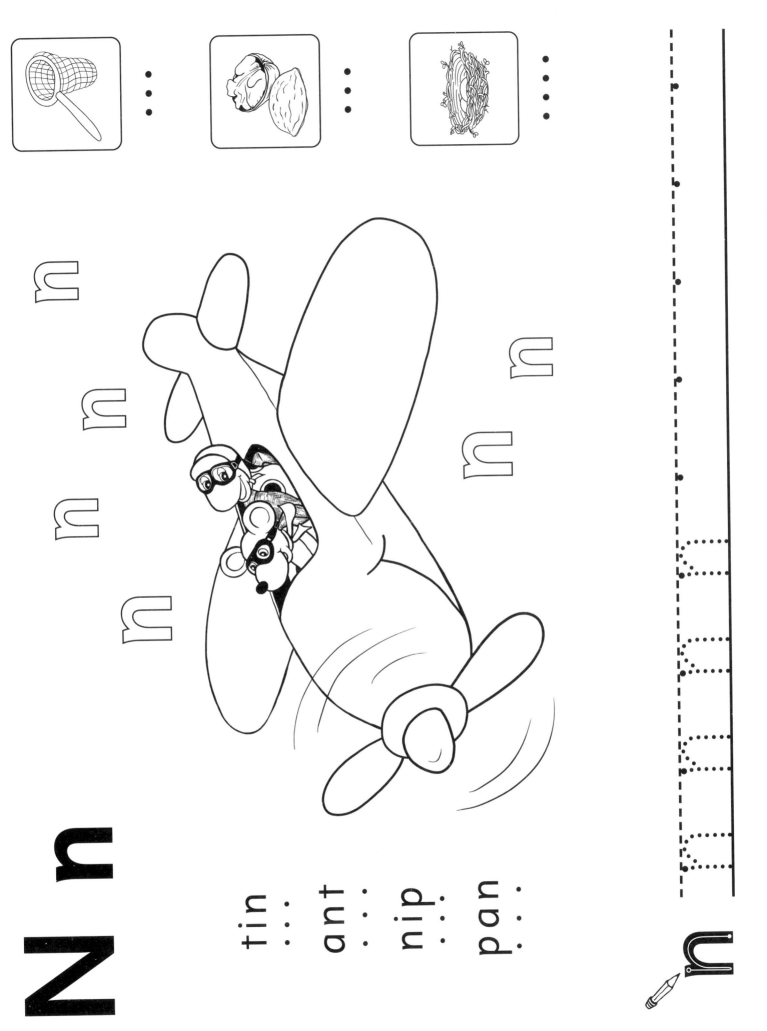

n n

n n

n n

n n

n n

tin : :
ant : :
nip : :
pan : :

n

Letter Sound: /c k/

Flashcards: Review the letter sounds already taught: /s/, /a/, /t/, /i/, /p/, /n/.

Storyline: Inky is visiting her cousins, who live in a castle in Spain. She is having a snack in the courtyard café when some Spanish dancers appear, clicking their castanets. They start to dance and clap to the music, swirling their bright crimson dresses. Inky jumps up and joins in, clicking her fingers in the air: "c, k, ck, ck!"

Action: The students pretend to play Spanish castanets and click their fingers in the air, saying c, k, ck, ck.

Letter formation: Explain how a caterpillar /c/ and a kicking /k/ are written, pointing out that kicking /k/ is a tall letter. The students form the letters in the air. Then they practice writing each letter on their sound sheets. They write over the dotted letters and then try again, using the starting dots. Several other letters begin with a caterpillar /c/ formation: ‹a›, ‹d›, ‹g›, ‹o›, ‹q›.

Blending: Blend the words on the sound sheet with the students: *kit, cap, pick, sack*. The students point to the dot underneath each sound as they say it. Explain that when two letters making the same sound are next to each other, you only say the sound once: /p-i-ck/ and /s-a-ck/, not /p-i-c-k/ and /s-a-c-k/. More words from the word bank can be written on the board for extra blending practice.

Identifying the sounds: This activity is for aural segmenting only. Look at the three small pictures on the sound sheet. Say the words and then sound them out with the students, holding up a finger for each sound: c-a-t, c-r-a-b, s-t-i-ck. Say the sounds again, pointing to the dots under the words. Do some more segmenting, using short words from the word bank.

Word bank: act, can, cap, cat, kin, kit, kick, kiss, pack, pick, sack, sick, tack, tick, scan, skip, skin, tact, snack, stack, stick, attic, panic, napkin, picnic; a sick cat.

Sound sheet: Encourage the students to form the letters correctly and to color the pictures neatly when completing the sound sheet.

Listen and write: Ask the students to write a caterpillar /c/ and a kicking /k/. Then call out the following words: *it, at*. For each one, ask the students to listen for the sounds and write the word. Afterward, sound out each word for the students, writing the letters on the board so that they can check their work.

Further ideas
• Sing the /ck/ song from Jolly Songs.
• Make a collage of cats and kittens.
• Make castanets from paper plates folded in half. Decorate plain plates or use patterned ones.
• Pin up the /ck/ section of the Wall Frieze.

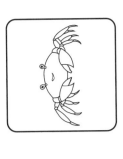 : : 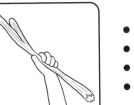 :

Cc Kk

ck

k

c

c

k

ck

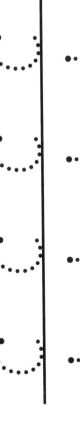

kit : : :

cap : :

pick : :

sack : :

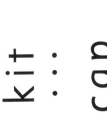  

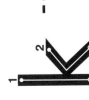

Letter Sound: /e/

Flashcards: Review the letter sounds already taught: /s/, /a/, /t/, /i/, /p/, /n/, /c/, /k/.

Storyline: A family is staying on a farm in the country. Every morning, the children get up early to fetch water from the well, feed the hens, and collect the eggs for breakfast. Back in the kitchen, they give the eggs to the farmer's wife. She cracks them open, tapping them on the side of a pan: "e, e, e, e."

 Action: The students pretend to crack open an egg. They tap with one hand saying *e, e, e,* and then mime opening the eggshell, saying *e.*

Letter formation: Explain how the letter for /e/ is written, pointing out that it is unusual because it does not start at or near the top of the letter, but halfway up. The students form the letter in the air. Then they practice writing the letter on their sound sheets. They write over the dotted letters and then try again, using the starting dots.

Blending: Blend the words on the sound sheet with the students: *ten, pet, tent, neck.* The students point to the dot underneath each sound as they say it. Remind them that when two letters making the same sound are next to each other, you only say the sound once: /n-e-ck/, not /n-e-c-k/. More words from the word bank can be written on the board for extra blending practice.

Identifying the sounds: This activity is for aural segmenting only. Look at the three small pictures on the sound sheet. Say the words and then sound them out with the students, holding up a finger for each sound: p-e-n, e-l-f, b-e-d. Say the sounds again, pointing to the dots under the words. Do some more segmenting, using short words from the word bank.

Word bank: net, pen, pet, set, ten, neck, peck, kept, nest, pest, sent, step, tent, test, speck, spent, tennis, insect, inspect; a pet cat.

Sound sheet: Encourage the students to form the letters correctly and to color the pictures neatly when completing the sound sheet.

Listen and write: Call out the sounds /e/, /c k/, /n/, /p/ and ask the students to write the letter for each one. Remind them that the sound /c k/ can be written as a caterpillar /c/ or a kicking /k/. Then call out the following words: *net, pen.* For each one, ask the students to listen for the sounds and write the word. Afterward, sound out each word for the students, writing the letters on the board so that they can check their work.

Further ideas
• Sing the /e/ song from Jolly Songs.
• Draw pictures of animals that hatch from eggs.
• Plant cress or mustard seeds in empty eggshells.
• Pin up the /e/ section of the Wall Frieze.

E e

ten : :
pet : :
tent : :
neck : :

🖍 e

Letter Sound: /h/

Flashcards: Review the letter sounds already taught: /s/, /a/, /t/, /i/, /p/, /n/, /c/, /k/, /e/.

Storyline: It is the school's summer fun day and the children are taking part in some races: running, jumping, and hopping. Inky Mouse and her friends are watching them and decide to have a hopping race themselves. Hopping is hard work on a hot day and by the time they have finished, they are huffing and puffing: "h, h, h, h!"

 Action: The students pretend to pant, holding their hand up to their mouth and saying *h, h, h, h.* They should be able to feel their breath on their hand as they do so.

Letter formation: Explain how the letter for /h/ is written, pointing out that it is a tall letter. The students form the letter in the air. Then they practice writing the letter on their sound sheets. They write over the dotted letters and then try again, using the starting dots.

Blending: Blend the words on the sound sheet with the students: *hip, hat, hen, hiss.* The students point to the dot underneath each sound as they say it. Remind them that when two letters making the same sound are next to each other, you only say the sound once: /h-i-ss/, not /h-i-s-s/. More words from the word bank can be written on the board for extra blending practice.

Identifying the sounds: This activity is for aural segmenting only. Look at the three small pictures on the sound sheet. Say the words and then sound them out with the students, holding up a finger for each sound: h-oo-k, h-or-se, h-a-n-d. Say the sounds again, pointing to the dots under the words. Do some more segmenting, using short words from the word bank.

Word bank: hat, hen, hip, hit, hiss, hint, hectic; a hen in a pen.

Sound sheet: Encourage the students to form the letters correctly and to color the pictures neatly when completing the sound sheet.

Listen and write: Call out the sounds /h/, /e/, /c k/, /n/ and ask the students to write the letter for each one. Remind them that the sound /c k/ can be written as a caterpillar /c/ or a kicking /k/. Then call out the following words: *hat, hen.* For each one, ask the students to listen for the sounds and write the word. Afterward, sound out each word for the students, writing the letters on the board so that they can check their work.

Further ideas
• Sing the /h/ song from Jolly Songs.
• Have a hopping race.
• Make pictures of hedgehogs with handprint prickles.
• Pin up the /h/ section of the Wall Frieze.

Hh

h h h
h h h
h

hip : :
hat : :
hen : :
hiss : :

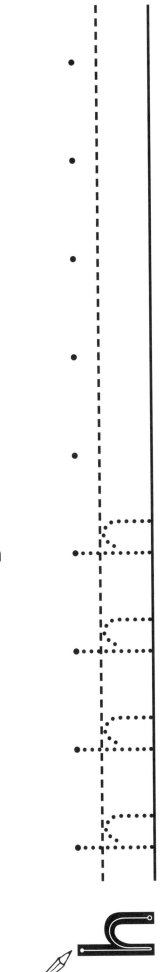

h

Letter Sound: /r/

Flashcards: Review the letter sounds already taught: /s/, /a/, /t/, /i/, /p/, /n/, /c/, /k/, /e/, /h/.

Storyline: A boy has a playful new puppy. The puppy is exploring the boy's room and finds an old blanket next to some roller skates. He grips the blanket in his teeth and shakes it from side to side: "rrrrrr!" The boy tries to take it away, but the puppy hangs on tightly until the blanket rips into rags. The puppy has a name now: Rags!

 Action: The students shake their heads, like a puppy with a rag, making a continuous /rrrrrr/ sound.

Letter formation: Explain how the letter for /r/ is written. The students form the letter in the air. Then they practice writing the letter on their sound sheets. They write over the dotted letters and then try again, using the starting dots.

Blending: Blend the words on the sound sheet with the students: *rip, rat, rest, trap.* The students point to the dot underneath each sound as they say it. More words from the word bank can be written on the board for extra blending practice.

Identifying the sounds: This activity is for aural segmenting only. Look at the three small pictures on the sound sheet. Say the words and then sound them out with the students, holding up a finger for each sound: r-u-g, r-ai-n, r-a-bb-i-t. Say the sounds again, pointing to the dots under the words. Do some more segmenting, using short words from the word bank.

Word bank: ran, rap, rat, rip, rack, rent, rest, risk, trap, trek, trip, crack, press, prick, track, trick, crept, crisp, print, scrap, strap, strip, stress, spirit, strict; cracks in a pan.

Sound sheet: Encourage the students to form the letters correctly and to color the pictures neatly when completing the sound sheet.

Listen and write: Call out the sounds /r/, /h/, /e/, /c k/ and ask the students to write the letter for each one. Remind them that the sound /c k/ can be written as a caterpillar /c/ or a kicking /k/. Then call out the following words: *rip, rat.* For each one, ask the students to listen for the sounds and write the word. Afterward, sound out each word for the students, writing the letters on the board so that they can check their work.

Further ideas
• Sing the /r/ song from Jolly Songs.
• Paint pictures of rockets.
• Use pieces of rag to make a dog collage.
• Pin up the /r/ section of the Wall Frieze.

R r

rip
rat
rest
trap

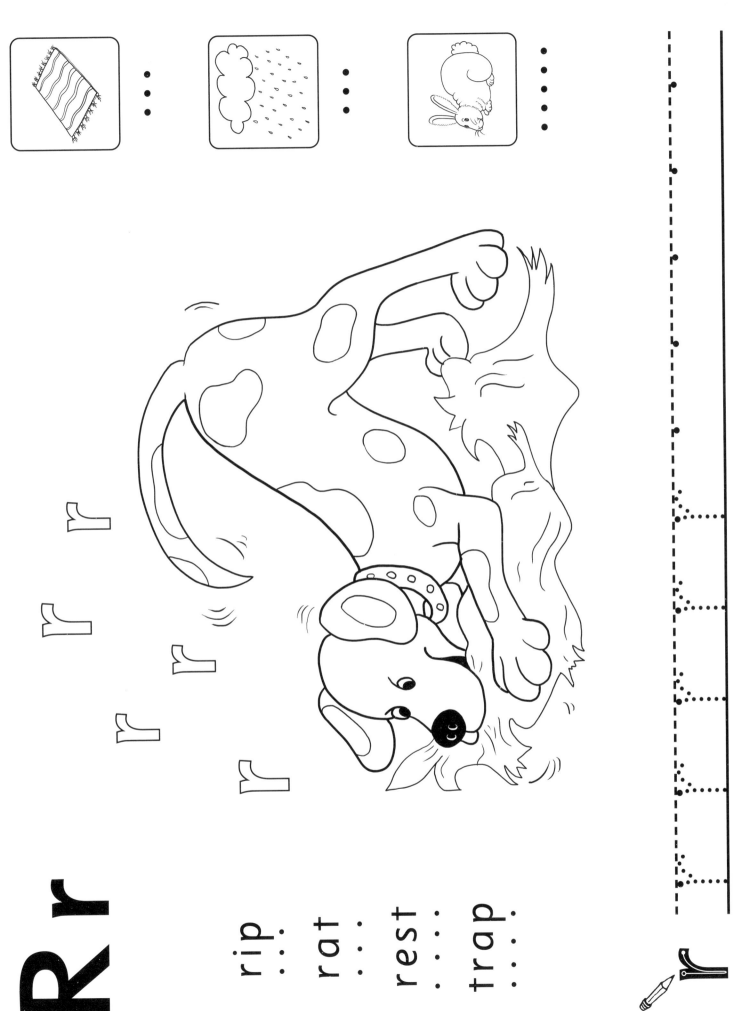

Letter Sound: /m/

Flashcards: Review the letter sounds already taught: /s/, /a/, /t/, /i/, /p/, /n/, /c/, /k/, /e/, /h/, /r/.

Storyline: A boy has invited some friends over for a meal. They think about the many meals they might have and which one they like most: maybe meatballs, tomato soup, or chicken and mushroom pie. The boy's mother brings in a large dish of lamb and peas. They all rub their tummies hungrily, saying "Mmmmmm!"

Action: The students rub their tummies and make a continuous /mmmmmm/ sound.

Letter formation: Explain how the letter for /m/ is written. The students form the letter in the air. Then they practice writing the letter on their sound sheets. They write over the dotted letters and then try again, using the starting dots.

Blending: Blend the words on the sound sheet with the students: *men, him, miss, man*. The students point to the dot underneath each sound as they say it. Remind them that when two letters making the same sound are next to each other, you only say the sound once: /m-i-ss/, not /m-i-s-s/. More words from the word bank can be written on the board for extra blending practice.

Identifying the sounds: This activity is for aural segmenting only. Look at the three small pictures on the sound sheet. Say the words and then sound them out with the students, holding up a finger for each sound: m-a-p, m-u-g, s-t-a-m-p. Say the sounds again, pointing to the dots under the words. Do some more segmenting, using short words from the word bank.

Word bank: hem, him, imp, man, map, mat, men, met, ram, rim, mass, mess, miss, camp, mint, mist, ramp, stem, trim, smack, mimic, stamp, tempt, tramp; a man in a hat.

Sound sheet: Encourage the students to form the letters correctly and to color the pictures neatly when completing the sound sheet.

Listen and write: Call out the sounds /m/, /r/, /h/, /e/ and ask the students to write the letter for each one. Then call out the following words: *map, rim*. For each one, ask the students to listen for the sounds and write the word. Afterward, sound out each word for the students, writing the letters on the board so that they can check their work.

Further ideas
• Sing the /m/ song from Jolly Songs.
• Make masks out of different materials.
• Make a collage of meals, sticking pictures from magazines onto paper plates.
• Pin up the /m/ section of the Wall Frieze.

M m

 :  :

m

m

m

m

m

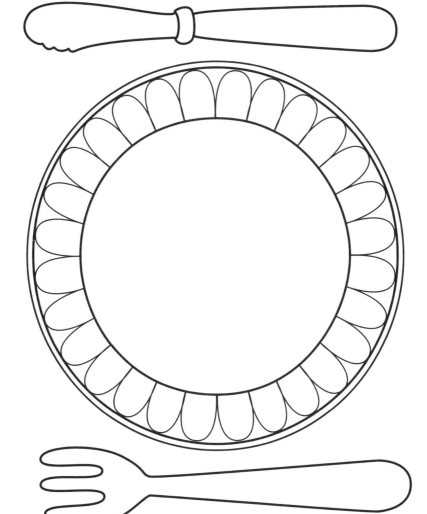

men
him
miss
man

Letter Sound: /d/

Flashcards: Review the letter sounds already taught: /s/, /a/, /t/, /i/, /p/, /n/, /c/, /k/, /e/, /h/, /r/, /m/.

Storyline: A boy is tidying his toy cupboard. He pulls out a teddy bear, his old donkey, a box of dominoes, and a duck. Next, he sees his yellow digger and takes it out for a drive. At the very back of the cupboard, he sees his old red and blue drum. He marches up and down, banging the drum: "d, d, d, d!"

 Action: The students pretend to be playing a drum, moving their hands up and down and saying *d, d, d, d.*

Letter formation: Explain how the letter for /d/ is written, pointing out that it starts with a caterpillar /c/ and is a tall letter. The students form the letter in the air. Then they practice writing the letter on their sound sheets. They write over the dotted letters and then try again, using the starting dots.

Blending: Blend the words on the sound sheet with the students: *dip, red, dad, hand.* The students point to the dot underneath each sound as they say it. More words from the word bank can be written on the board for extra blending practice.

Identifying the sounds: This activity is for aural segmenting only. Look at the three small pictures on the sound sheet. Say the words and then sound them out with the students, holding up a finger for each sound: d-o-g, d-r-e-ss, d-e-s-k. Say the sounds again, pointing to the dots under the words. Do some more segmenting, using short words from the word bank.

Word bank: add, and, dad, den, did, dim, din, dip, end, had, hid, kid, mad, pad, red, rid, sad, deck, damp, dent, desk, disk, drip, hand, sand, mend, send, skid, tend, dress, spend, stand, timid, intend, dentist, drastic, handstand; a red dress.

Sound sheet: Encourage the students to form the letters correctly and to color the pictures neatly when completing the sound sheet.

Listen and write: Call out the sounds /d/, /m/, /r/, /h/ and ask the students to write the letter for each one. Then call out the following words: *sad, dip.* For each one, ask the students to listen for the sounds and write the word. Afterward, sound out each word for the students, writing the letters on the board so that they can check their work.

Further ideas
• Sing the /d/ song from Jolly Songs.
• Make model dinosaurs from modeling clay.
• Play a game of dominoes.
• Pin up the /d/ section of the Wall Frieze.

Extra support: Now is a good time to assess and identify any students who are struggling to remember the letter sounds, blend words, write letters, or identify the sounds in words. Early intervention is extremely important. See pages 17 to 19 for more information.

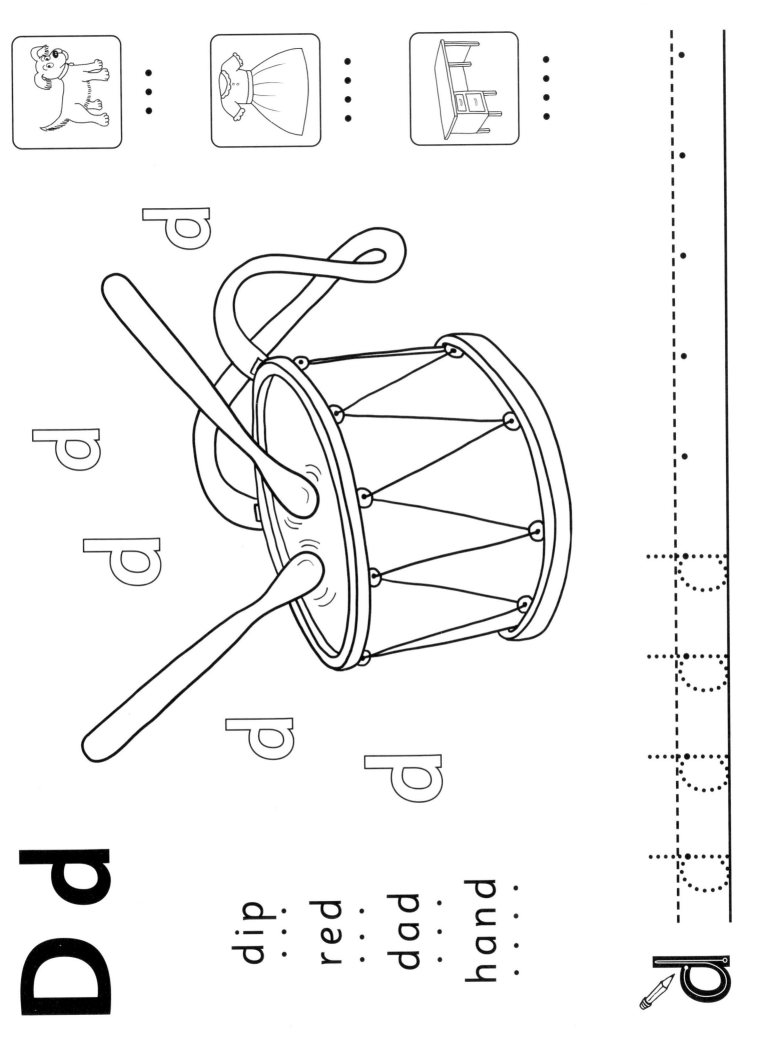

D d

d d d d d

d

dip
red
dad
hand

Letter Sound: /g/

Flashcards: Review the letter sounds already taught: /s/, /a/, /t/, /i/, /p/, /n/, /c/, /k/, /e/, /h/, /r/, /m/, /d/.

Storyline: A girl is staying with her grandmother. She checks on the geese and the goat in the garden, and then goes to wash her hands. "Granny," she cries, "the sink is blocked and full of water." Granny calls the plumber. When the sink is unblocked, the water gurgles down the drain: "g, g, g, g."

 Action: The students pretend their hand is water spiraling down a drain and say *g, g, g, g.*

Letter formation: Explain how the letter for /g/ is written, pointing out that it starts with a caterpillar /c/ and has a tail that goes down under the line. The students form the letter in the air. Then they practice writing the letter on their sound sheets. They write over the dotted letters and then try again, using the starting dots.

Blending: Blend the words on the sound sheet with the students: *egg, dig, peg, grin.* The students point to the dot underneath each sound as they say it. More words from the word bank can be written on the board for extra blending practice.

Identifying the sounds: This activity is for aural segmenting only. Look at the three small pictures on the sound sheet. Say the words and then sound them out with the students, holding up a finger for each sound: g-l-a-ss, g-oa-t, p-l-u-g. Say the sounds again, pointing to the dots under the words. Do some more segmenting, using short words from the word bank.

Word bank: egg, dig, gap, gas, get, nag, peg, rag, rig, sag, tag, crag, drag, gram, grid, grim, grin, grip, snag, stag, grand, granddad; granddad is sad.

Sound sheet: Encourage the students to form the letters correctly and to color the pictures neatly when completing the sound sheet.

Listen and write: Call out the sounds /g/, /d/, /m/, /r/ and ask the students to write the letter for each one. Then call out the following words: *sag, peg, dig, get.* For each one, ask the students to listen for the sounds and write the word. Afterward, sound out each word for the students, writing the letters on the board so that they can check their work.

Further ideas
• Sing the /g/ song from Jolly Songs.
• Paint pictures of green frogs.
• Read the story of The Three Billy Goats Gruff.
• Pin up the /g/ section of the Wall Frieze.

G g

egg
dig
peg
grin

g g g
g g
g g

Letter Sound: /o/

Flashcards: Review the letter sounds already taught: /s/, /a/, /t/, /i/, /p/, /n/, /c/, /k/, /e/, /h/, /r/, /m/, /d/, /g/.

Storyline: A family has moved into a new house, with bunk beds in the children's bedroom. The sister has the top bunk and the brother has the bottom bunk. When they go to bed, the brother is not sleepy. He plays with his toy octopus, turning the light on and off, on and off: "o-o, o-o."

 Action: The students point their finger as if pushing a wall switch on and off and say *o-o, o-o.*

Letter formation: Explain how the letter for /o/ is written, pointing out that it starts with a caterpillar /c/. The students form the letter in the air. Then they practice writing the letter on their sound sheets. They write over the dotted letters and then try again, using the starting dots.

Blending: Blend the words on the sound sheet with the students: *hot, dog, hop, socks.* The students point to the dot underneath each sound as they say it. More words from the word bank can be written on the board for extra blending practice.

Identifying the sounds: This activity is for aural segmenting only. Look at the three small pictures on the sound sheet. Say the words and then sound them out with the students, holding up a finger for each sound: d-o-ll, r-o-ck, o-tt-er. Say the sounds again, pointing to the dots under the words. Do some more segmenting, using short words from the word bank.

Word bank: on, odd, cod, cog, cot, dog, dot, got, hop, hot, mop, nod, not, pod, pop, pot, rod, rot, top, dock, mock, rock, sock, crop, drop, pond, spot, stop, trod, trot, cross, comic, topic, cannot, tick-tock, desktop; a rock in a pond.

Sound sheet: Encourage the students to form the letters correctly and to color the pictures neatly when completing the sound sheet.

Listen and write: Call out the sounds /o/, /g/, /d/, /m/ and ask the students to write the letter for each one. Then call out the following words: *hop, dot, nod, cog.* For each one, ask the students to listen for the sounds and write the word. Afterward, sound out each word for the students, writing the letters on the board so that they can check their work.

Further ideas
• Sing the /o/ song from Jolly Songs.
• Make an octopus with paper-chain tentacles.
• Create patterns of ‹o› shapes, printed on paper using the end of cardboard tubes.
• Pin up the /o/ section of the Wall Frieze.

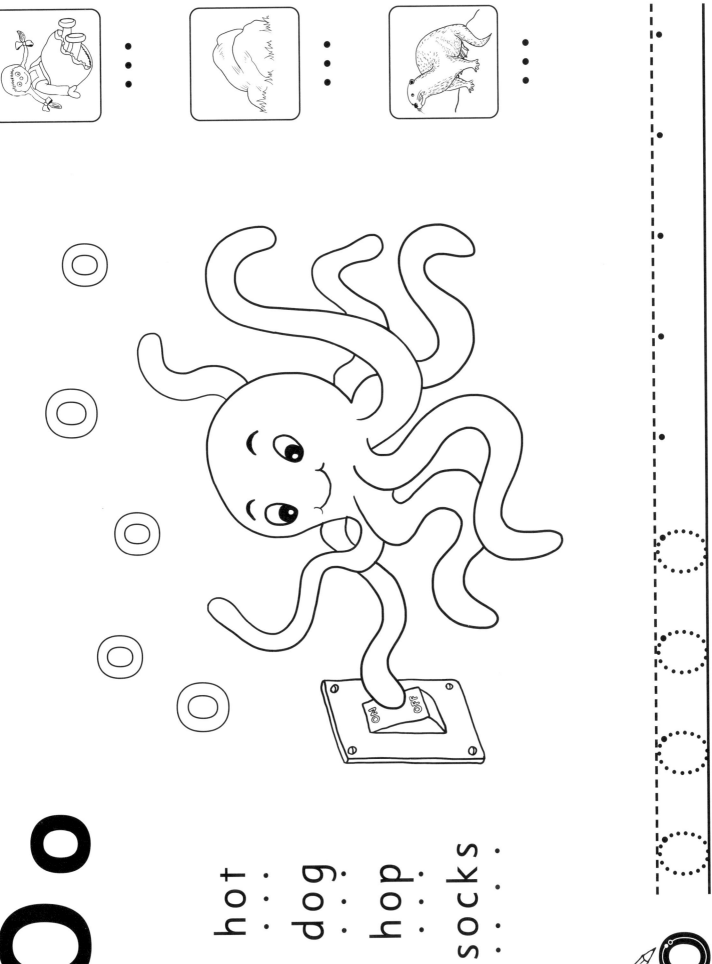

Oo

hot
dog
hop
socks

Letter Sound: /u/

Flashcards: Review the letter sounds already taught: /s/, /a/, /t/, /i/, /p/, /n/, /c/, /k/, /e/, /h/, /r/, /m/, /d/, /g/, /o/.

Storyline: A family goes out for a walk. It is very sunny, but the children insist on taking their new umbrellas. Everyone laughs until some big black clouds appear on the horizon. Soon it is pouring with rain! Everyone else gets wet, but the children stay nice and dry as they put up their umbrellas: "u, u, u, u."

 Action: The students pretend to hold an umbrella and put it up, saying *u, u, u, u.*

Letter formation: Explain how the letter for /u/ is written. The students form the letter in the air. Then they practice writing the letter on their sound sheets. They write over the dotted letters and then try again, using the starting dots.

Blending: Blend the words on the sound sheet with the students: *up, sun, mud, truck.* The students point to the dot underneath each sound as they say it. More words from the word bank can be written on the board for extra blending practice.

Identifying the sounds: This activity is for aural segmenting only. Look at the three small pictures on the sound sheet. Say the words and then sound them out with the students, holding up a finger for each sound: c-u-p, d-u-ck, d-r-u-m. Say the sounds again, pointing to the dots under the words. Do some more segmenting, using short words from the word bank.

Word bank: up, us, cup, cut, dug, gum, hug, hum, hut, mud, mug, nun, nut, pun, pup, rug, run, rut, sum, sun, tug, duck, muck, putt, suck, tuck, drug, drum, dump, dusk, dust, gust, hump, hunt, must, pump, rump, rust, snug, spun, tusk, stuck, truck, crust, grunt, mumps, stump, trust, undid, upset, eggcup, hiccup, sunset, suntan, discuss, rucksack, undress, product, pumpkin, instruct; a red sunset.

Sound sheet: Encourage the students to form the letters correctly and to color the pictures neatly when completing the sound sheet.

Listen and write: Call out the sounds /u/, /o/, /g/, /d/ and ask the students to write the letter for each one. Then call out the following words: *run, sum, cut, hug.* For each one, ask the students to listen for the sounds and write the word. Afterward, sound out each word for the students, writing the letters on the board so that they can check their work.

Further ideas
• Sing the /u/ song from Jolly Songs.
• Make umbrella mobiles with cut-out raindrops.
• Paint umbrellas in different patterns and make a collage.
• Pin up the /u/ section of the Wall Frieze.

U u

: : : :

up ·
sun : ·
mud : · :
truck : : : :

Letter Sound: /l/

Flashcards: Review the letter sounds already taught: /s/, /a/, /t/, /i/, /p/, /n/, /c/, /k/, /e/, /h/, /r/, /m/, /d/, /g/, /o/, /u/.

Storyline: Inky and her friends are having a party. There are lots of balloons and some lovely food. Bee likes the little cakes and the lemonade. They play some party games, starting with Sleeping Lions. Then Snake wins Pin the Tail on the Donkey and gets a lime lollipop as a prize. He licks his lollipop: "lllll."

 Action: The students pretend to lick a lollipop, sticking out their tongues and making a continuous /lllll/ sound.

Letter formation: Explain how the letter for /l/ is written, pointing out that it is a tall letter. The students form the letter in the air. Then they practice writing the letter on their sound sheets. They write over the dotted letters and then try again, using the starting dots.

Blending: Blend the words on the sound sheet with the students: *leg, lips, doll, help.* The students point to the dot underneath each sound as they say it. More words from the word bank can be written on the board for extra blending practice.

Identifying the sounds: This activity is for aural segmenting only. Look at the three small pictures on the sound sheet. Say the words and then sound them out with the students, holding up a finger for each sound: l-o-g, l-a-m-p, b-e-ll. Say the sounds again, pointing to the dots under the words. Do some more segmenting, using short words from the word bank.

Word bank: ill, elk, lad, lap, led, leg, let, lid, lip, lit, log, lot, pal, dill, doll, dull, gill, gull, hill, kill, lass, less, lick, lock, loss, luck, mill, pill, sell, sill, tell, till, clap, clip, clog, glad, glum, gulp, held, help, kilt, lamp, land, lend, lent, limp, list, lost, lump, melt, milk, plan, plop, plot, plug, plum, plus, silk, slam, slap, slid, slim, slip, slit, slot, slug, sulk, tilt, click, clock, skill, skull, smell, spell, spill, still, adult, clamp, clump, halal, limit, plump, slept, spelt, spilt, split, solid, until, unless, unlock, insult, stilts, laptop, unplug, plastic, lipstick, clarinet, splendid; a lost dog.

Sound sheet: Encourage the students to form the letters correctly and to color the pictures neatly when completing the sound sheet.

Listen and write: Call out the sounds /l/, /u/, /o/, /g/ and ask the students to write the letter for each one. Then call out the following words: *lap, lot, leg, lid.* For each one, ask the students to listen for the sounds and write the word. Afterward, sound out each word for the students, writing the letters on the board so that they can check their work.

Further ideas
• Sing the /l/ song from Jolly Songs.
• Make lemonade.
• Paint pictures of lollipops.
• Pin up the /l/ section of the Wall Frieze.

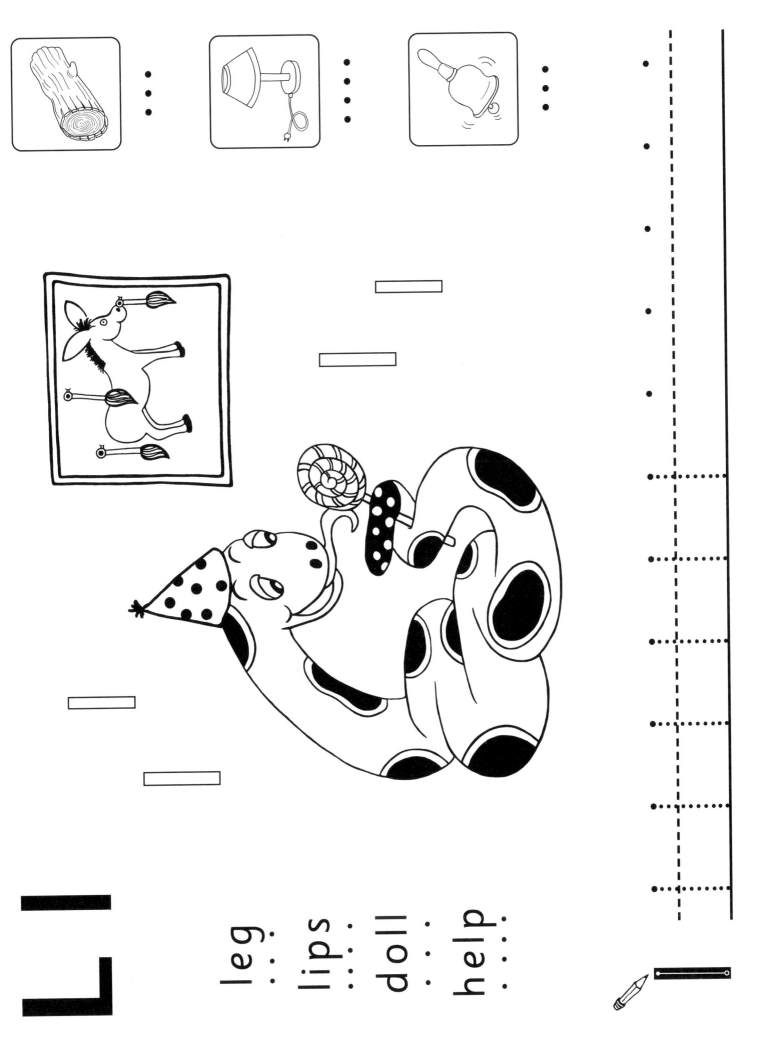

L l

leg
lips
doll
help

Letter Sound: /f/

Flashcards: Review the letter sounds already taught: /s/, /a/, /t/, /i/, /p/, /n/, /c/, /k/, /e/, /h/, /r/, /m/, /d/, /g/, /o/, /u/, /l/.

Storyline: A family is having a day at the beach. The children put on their flippers and play in the water with their large, floating inflatable fish. Then they build a sandcastle and put flags on the four towers. Suddenly, they hear a strange sound – the plug has come out of the inflatable fish and all the air is escaping: "ffffff."

 **Action:** The students slowly bring their hands together to mime an inflatable fish deflating, making a continuous /ffffffff/ sound.

Letter formation: Explain how the letter for /f/ is written, pointing out that it is a tall letter. The students form the letter in the air. Then they practice writing the letter on their sound sheets. They write over the dotted letters and then try again, using the starting dots.

Blending: Blend the words on the sound sheet with the students: *fit, fun, puff, soft.* The students point to the dot underneath each sound as they say it. More words from the word bank can be written on the board for extra blending practice.

Identifying the sounds: This activity is for aural segmenting only. Look at the three small pictures on the sound sheet. Say the words and then sound them out with the students, holding up a finger for each sound: f-a-n, f-l-a-g, f-r-o-g. Say the sounds again, pointing to the dots under the words. Do some more segmenting, using short words from the word bank.

Word bank: if, off, elf, fan, fat, fed, fig, fin, fit, fog, fun, cuff, fell, fill, fuss, huff, puff, tiff, fact, felt, film, fist, flag, flan, flap, flat, flip, flop, fond, font, frog, from, fund, gift, golf, left, lift, loft, self, sift, soft, tuft, cliff, flick, flock, fluff, frock, gruff, sniff, stiff, drift, frost, muffin, puffin, infect, traffic, frantic, himself, fantastic; a fat frog on a log.

Sound sheet: Encourage the students to form the letters correctly and to color the pictures neatly when completing the sound sheet.

Listen and write: Call out the sounds /f/, /l/, /u/, /o/ and ask the students to write the letter for each one. Then call out the following words: *fan, fit, fog, elf.* For each one, ask the students to listen for the sounds and write the word. Afterward, sound out each word for the students, writing the letters on the board so that they can check their work.

Further ideas
• Sing the /f/ song from Jolly Songs.
• Find out about different types of fish.
• Make a model aquarium with foil fish.
• Pin up the /f/ section of the Wall Frieze.

F f

fit

fun

puff

soft

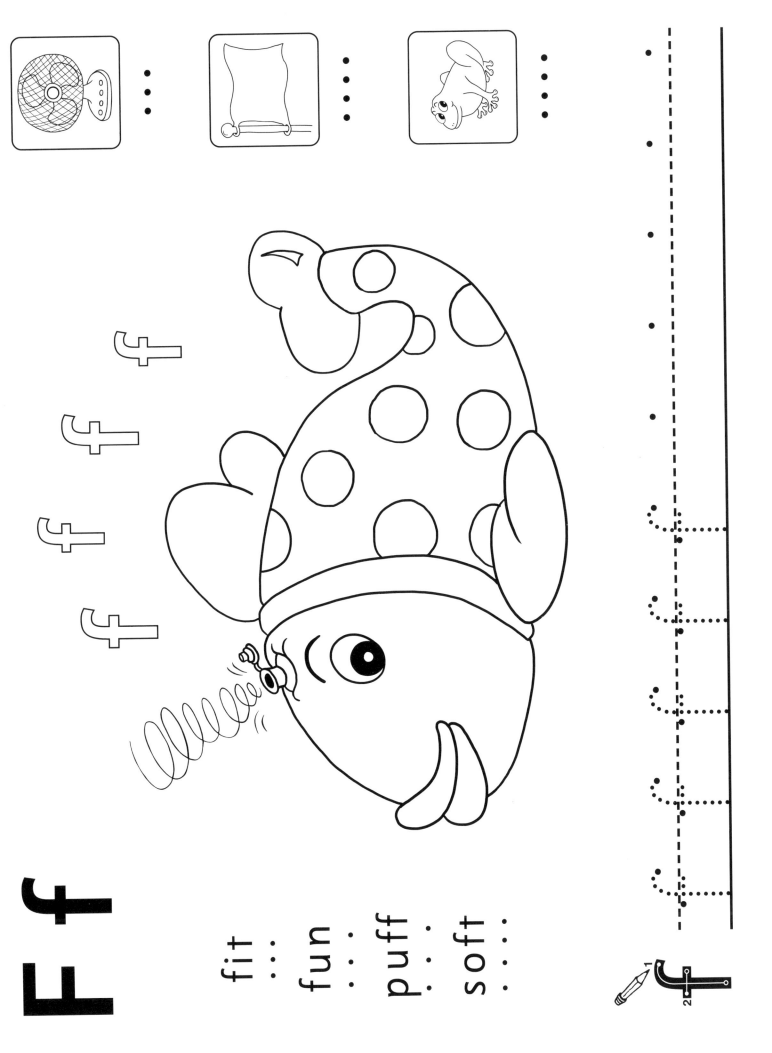

Letter Sound: /b/

Flashcards: Review the letter sounds already taught: /s/, /a/, /t/, /i/, /p/, /n/, /c/, /k/, /e/, /h/, /r/, /m/, /d/, /g/, /o/, /u/, /l/, /f/.

Storyline: Inky and her friends are in the park. They are on the bridge over the boating lake, throwing bread to the ducks. An old lady with a baby sits on a bench nearby, watching some children play baseball. Inky gets out her bat and ball too. Inky, Snake, and Bee take it in turns to throw the ball and bash it with the bat: "b, b, b, b."

 Action: The students pretend to hold a bat and hit a ball, saying *b, b, b, b*.

Letter formation: Explain how the letter for /b/ is written, pointing out that it is a tall letter that goes down the "bat" and bounces up and around the "ball." The students form the letter in the air. Then they practice writing the letter on their sound sheets. They write over the dotted letters and then try again, using the starting dots.

Blending: Blend the words on the sound sheet with the students: *big, bag, bell, crab.* The students point to the dot underneath each sound as they say it. More words from the word bank can be written on the board for extra blending practice.

Identifying the sounds: This activity is for aural segmenting only. Look at the three small pictures on the sound sheet. Say the words and then sound them out with the students, holding up a finger for each sound: b-e-l-t, b-a-t, w-e-b. Say the sounds again, pointing to the dots under the words. Do some more segmenting, using short words from the word bank.

Word bank: bad, bag, ban, bat, bed, beg, bet, bib, big, bin, bit, bud, bug, bun, bus, but, cab, cub, pub, rob, rub, back, bell, bill, boss, buck, belt, bend, bent, best, bulb, bump, club, crab, crib, grab, grub, scab, black, block, brick, blend, blond, habit, robin, rabbit; a big red bus.

Sound sheet: Encourage the students to form the letters correctly and to color the pictures neatly when completing the sound sheet.

Listen and write: Call out the sounds /b/, /f/, /l/, /u/ and ask the students to write the letter for each one. Then call out the following words: *bed, bus, bat, bib.* For each one, ask the students to listen for the sounds and write the word. Afterward, sound out each word for the students, writing the letters on the board so that they can check their work.

Further ideas
- Sing the /b/ song from Jolly Songs.
- Go on a bug hunt.
- Play games with a bat and ball.
- Pin up the /b/ section of the Wall Frieze.

Extra support: Remember to assess and identify any students who are struggling and provide them with the extra support they need. See pages 17 to 19 for more information.

Bb

b b

b

b b

b

big :
bag :
bell :
crab :

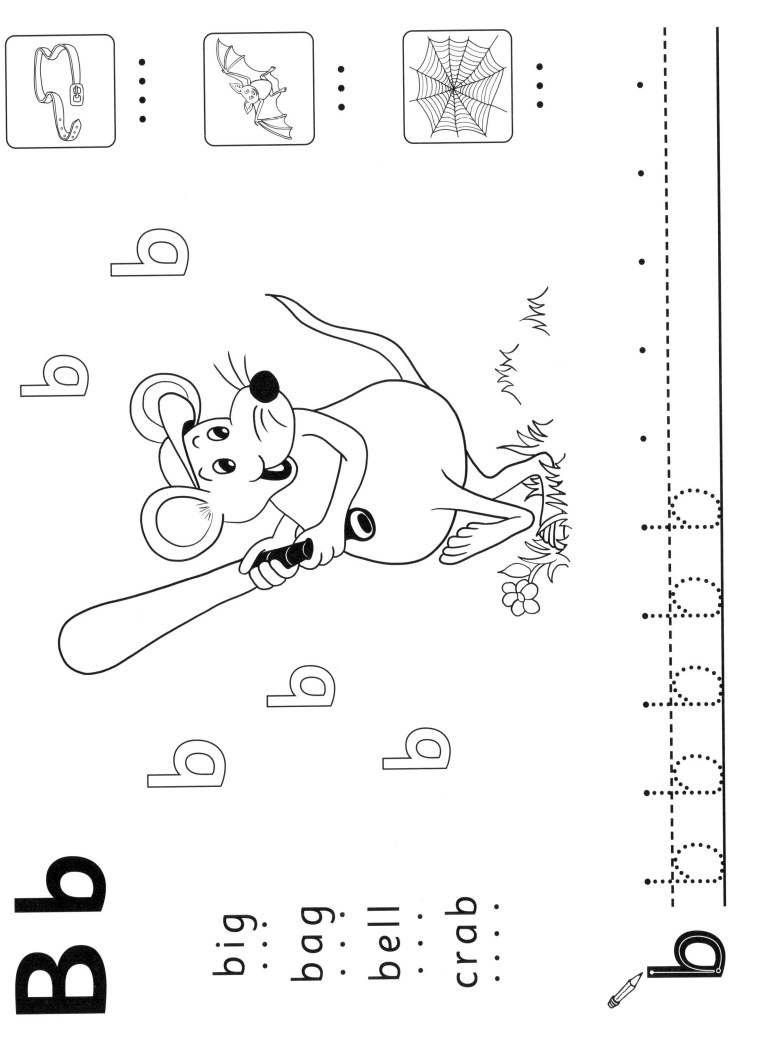

b b b b b

b

Letter Sound: /ai/

Flashcards: Review the letter sounds already taught: /s/, /a/, /t/, /i/, /p/, /n/, /c/, /k/, /e/, /h/, /r/, /m/, /d/, /g/, /o/, /u/, /l/, /f/, /b/.

Storyline: Bee is having trouble with her hearing. She keeps putting her hand to her ear and saying, "ai?" again and again. In the doctor's waiting room, she plays with a whale, a train, and a sailboat. Doctor Ail looks in her ears and finds lots of wax, so she gives Bee some eardrops. Now the wax has gone she doesn't say "ai?" anymore.

 Action: The students cup one hand over their ear, as if they are trying to hear something, and say *ai?*

Letter formation: The sound /ai/ is written with two letters. When two letters make one sound it is called a digraph. Remind the students how both letters are formed. The students form the letters for the digraph in the air. Then they practice writing them on their sound sheets.

Blending: Blend the words on the sound sheet with the students: *rain, tail, snail, paint.* The students point to the dot underneath each sound as they say it. More words from the word bank can be written on the board for extra blending practice.

Identifying the sounds: This activity is for aural segmenting only. Look at the three small pictures on the sound sheet. Say the words and then sound them out with the students, holding up a finger for each sound: ch-ai-n, n-ai-l, t-r-ai-n. Say the sounds again, pointing to the dots under the words. Do some more segmenting, using short words from the word bank.

Word bank: aid, ail, aim, bait, fail, gain, hail, laid, maid, mail, main, nail, paid, pail, pain, raid, rail, rain, sail, tail, brain, claim, drain, faint, grain, paint, plain, saint, snail, stain, trail, train, sprain, strain, raindrop; a snail trail.

Sound sheet: Encourage the students to form the letters correctly and to color the pictures neatly when completing the sound sheet.

Listen and write: Call out the sounds /ai/, /b/, /f/, /l/ and ask the students to write the letter(s) for each one. Then call out the following words: *aim, rail, pain, bait.* For each one, ask the students to listen for the sounds and write the word. Afterward, sound out each word for the students, writing the letters on the board so that they can check their work.

Further ideas
• Sing the /ai/ song from Jolly Songs.
• Make model snails from modeling clay.
• Paint rainy-day pictures on raindrop shapes.
• Pin up the /ai/ section of the Wall Frieze.

ai

ai   ai   ai

ai   ai

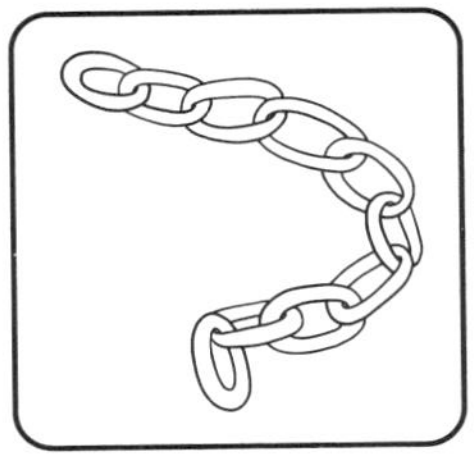

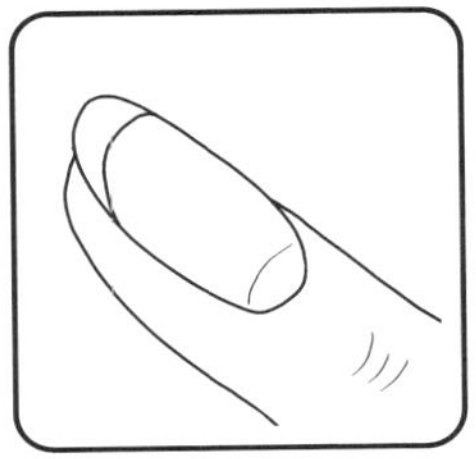

rain
tail
snail
paint

ai

Letter Sound: /j/

Flashcards: Review the letter sounds already taught: /s/, /a/, /t/, /i/, /p/, /n/, /c/, /k/, /e/, /h/, /r/, /m/, /d/, /g/, /o/, /u/, /l/, /f/, /b/, /ai/.

Storyline: A mother and her daughter have made some jello. When it is ready, they tip it carefully onto a plate. It is tall and red, with four layers. As they carry the giant jello to the table, it jiggles and joggles on the plate. The little girl laughs and wobbles just like the jello, saying: "j, j, j, j."

 Action: The students wobble like jello, saying *j, j, j, j.*

Letter formation: Explain how the letter for /j/ is written, pointing out that it has a tail that goes down under the line. The students form the letter in the air. Then they practice writing the letter on their sound sheets. They write over the dotted letters and then try again, using the starting dots.

Blending: Blend the words on the sound sheet with the students: *jet, jog, just, jump.* The students point to the dot underneath each sound as they say it. More words from the word bank can be written on the board for extra blending practice.

Identifying the sounds: This activity is for aural segmenting only. Look at the three small pictures on the sound sheet. Say the words and then sound them out with the students, holding up a finger for each sound: j-ar, j-a-m, j-ui-ce. Say the sounds again, pointing to the dots under the words. Do some more segmenting, using short words from the word bank.

Word bank: jab, jam, jet, jig, job, jog, jot, jug, jut, jack, jail, jump, just, object, project, subject; a traffic jam.

Sound sheet: Encourage the students to form the letters correctly and to color the pictures neatly when completing the sound sheet.

Listen and write: Call out the sounds /j/, /ai/, /b/, /f/ and ask the students to write the letter(s) for each one. Then call out the following words: *jet, job, jam, jug.* For each one, ask the students to listen for the sounds and write the word. Afterward, sound out each word for the students, writing the letters on the board so that they can check their work.

Further ideas
• Sing the /j/ song from Jolly Songs.
• Make some multicolored jello.
• Make a jellyfish with a paper-cup body and crêpe-paper tentacles.
• Pin up the /j/ section of the Wall Frieze.

J j

jet
jog
just
jump

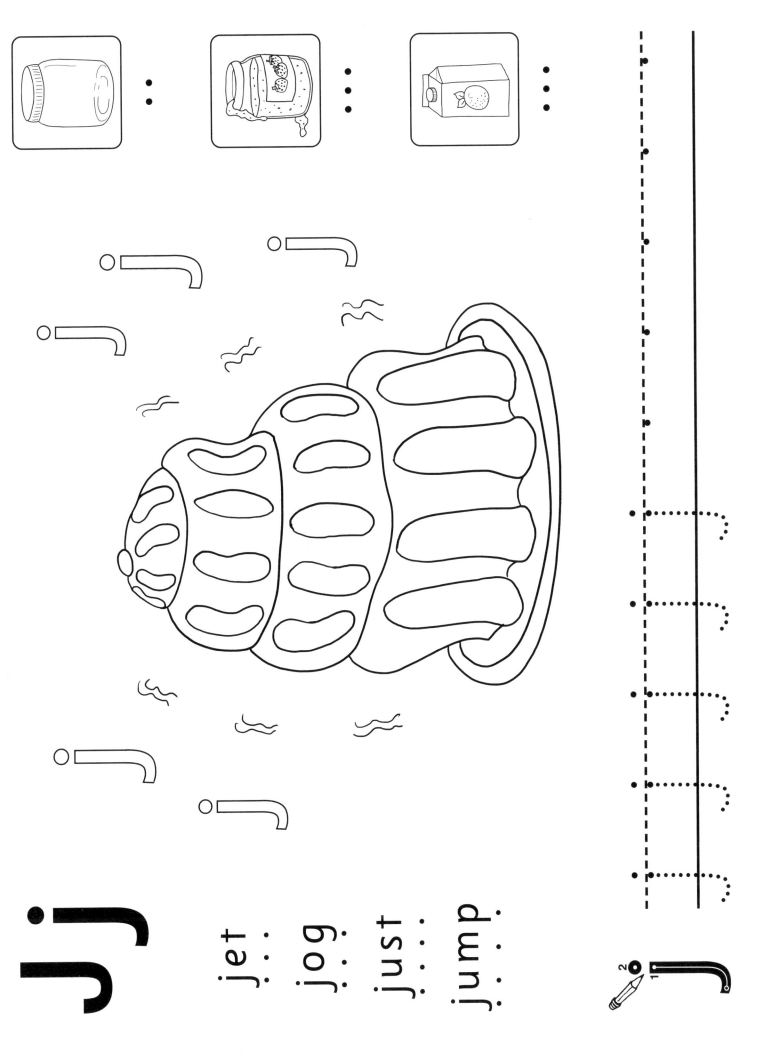

Letter Sound: /oa/

Flashcards: Review the letter sounds already taught: /s/, /a/, /t/, /i/, /p/, /n/, /c/, /k/, /e/, /h/, /r/, /m/, /d/, /g/, /o/, /u/, /l/, /f/, /b/, /ai/, /j/.

Storyline: A goat is very angry because the birds and squirrels in the oak tree are stealing his oats. He snorts at them and stamps his hooves, but they still ignore him. Finally, he charges and butts the oak tree. CRASH! The tree falls on the poor goat. "Oh, no!" says Inky, who is passing by. "Don't worry. I'll ask the farmer to rescue you!"

 Action: The students cover their mouth with one hand as if something is wrong and say *oa!*

Letter formation: The sound /oa/ is written with two letters. When two letters make one sound it is called a digraph. Remind the students how both letters are formed. The students form the letters for the digraph in the air. Then they practice writing them on their sound sheets.

Blending: Blend the words on the sound sheet with the students: *goat, road, soap, toast.* The students point to the dot underneath each sound as they say it. More words from the word bank can be written on the board for extra blending practice.

Identifying the sounds: This activity is for aural segmenting only. Look at the three small pictures on the sound sheet. Say the words and then sound them out with the students, holding up a finger for each sound: c-oa-t, t-oa-d, b-oa-t. Say the sounds again, pointing to the dots under the words. Do some more segmenting, using short words from the word bank.

Word bank: oak, boat, coal, coat, foal, foam, goal, goat, load, loaf, moan, moat, oats, road, roam, soak, soap, toad, boast, cloak, coast, croak, float, groan, roast, toast, unload, raincoat; A toad croaks.

Sound sheet: Encourage the students to form the letters correctly and to color the pictures neatly when completing the sound sheet.

Listen and write: Call out the sounds /oa/, /j/, /ai/, /b/ and ask the students to write the letter(s) for each one. Then call out the following words: *coat, loaf, moan, soap.* For each one, ask the students to listen for the sounds and write the word. Afterward, sound out each word for the students, writing the letters on the board so that they can check their work.

Further ideas
• Sing the /oa/ song from Jolly Songs.
• Read about different types of toads.
• Make paper boats and see if they float.
• Pin up the /oa/ section of the Wall Frieze.

oa

goat
road
soap
toast

oa

oa

oa

oa

Letter Sound: /ie/

Flashcards: Review the letter sounds already taught: /s/, /a/, /t/, /i/, /p/, /n/, /c/, /k/, /e/, /h/, /r/, /m/, /d/, /g/, /o/, /u/, /l/, /f/, /b/, /ai/, /j/, /oa/.

Storyline: Snake needs to find a costume to wear to a party. He cannot decide whether to go as a diver, a lifeguard, a tightrope walker, or a sailor. Eventually, he decides that being a sailor is best. He finds a sailor's hat and practices his salute, standing to attention and saying, "ie, ie!"

 Action: The students pretend to be sailors and salute, saying *ie, ie.*

Letter formation: The sound /ie/ is written with two letters. When two letters make one sound it is called a digraph. Remind the students how both letters are formed. The students form the letters for the digraph in the air. Then they practice writing them on their sound sheets.

Blending: Blend the words on the sound sheet with the students: *lie, tied, untie, magpie.* The students point to the dot underneath each sound as they say it. More words from the word bank can be written on the board for extra blending practice.

Identifying the sounds: This activity is for aural segmenting only. Look at the three small pictures on the sound sheet. Say the words and then sound them out with the students, holding up a finger for each sound: p-ie, t-ie, f-l-ie-s. Say the sounds again, pointing to the dots under the words. Do some more segmenting, using short words from the word bank.

Word bank: die, lie, pie, tie, died, lied, tied, cried, dried, fried, spied, tried, untie, magpie, untied, terrified; a fried egg.

Sound sheet: Encourage the students to form the letters correctly and to color the pictures neatly when completing the sound sheet.

Listen and write: Call out the sounds /ie/, /oa/, /j/, /ai/ and ask the students to write the letter(s) for each one. Then call out the following words: *pie, tie, lie, die.* For each one, ask the students to listen for the sounds and write the word. Afterward, sound out each word for the students, writing the letters on the board so that they can check their work.

Further ideas
• Sing the /ie/ song from Jolly Songs.
• Decorate cut-out paper ties.
• Create symmetrical butterflies. Paint half the body and one wing, fold the paper over, rub, and unfold.
• Pin up the /ie/ section of the Wall Frieze.

ie

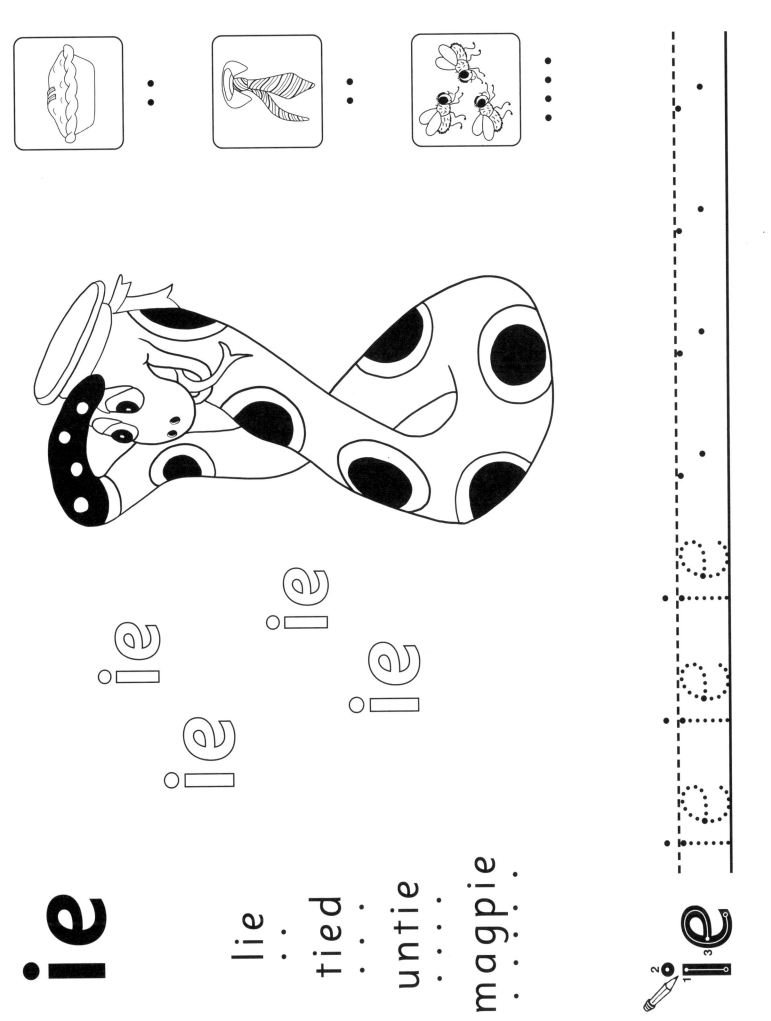

lie

tied

untie

magpie

Letter Sounds: /ee/ and /or/

Flashcards: Review the letter sounds already taught: /s/, /a/, /t/, /i/, /p/, /n/, /c/, /k/, /e/, /h/, /r/, /m/, /d/, /g/, /o/, /u/, /l/, /f/, /b/, /ai/, /j/, /oa/, /ie/.

Storyline: A donkey lives with a horse and some sheep next to a cornfield. One August morning, some children come to see him. They like to talk to him and feed him carrots. The donkey is always pleased to see the children. He gives them his usual cheery greeting, waggling his ears up and down, braying "ee-or!"

 Action: The students put their hands on their head like a donkey's ears and say *ee*, pointing their hands up, and then *or*, pointing them down.

Letter formation: The sounds /ee/ and /or/ are both written with two letters. When two letters make one sound it is called a digraph. Remind the students how the letters in each digraph are formed. The students form the letters for each digraph in the air. Then they practice writing them on their sound sheets.

Blending: Blend the words on the sound sheet with the students: *bee, tree, sleep; corn, fork, storm.* The students point to the dot underneath each sound as they say it. More words from the word bank can be written on the board for extra blending practice.

Identifying the sounds: This activity is for aural segmenting only. Look at the three small pictures on the sound sheet. Say the words and then sound them out with the students, holding up a finger for each sound: sh-ee-p, h-or-n, s-ee-s-aw. Say the sounds again, pointing to the dots under the words. Do some more segmenting, using short words from the word bank.

Word bank:

/ee/: bee, eel, see, beef, been, deep, feed, feel, feet, free, heel, jeep, keen, keep, leek, meet, need, peek, peel, peep, reef, reel, seed, seek, seem, seen, tree, bleed, creek, creep, greed, green, greet, sleep, speed, steel, steep, coffee, settee, toffee, screen, street, indeed, canteen: a deep sleep.
/or/: or, for, born, cord, cork, corn, fork, form, fort, horn, lord, port, sort, torn, snort, sport, stork, storm, inform, foghorn, popcorn, portrait, landlord, platform; a fork in a road.

Sound sheet: Encourage the students to form the letters correctly and to color the pictures neatly when completing the sound sheet.

Listen and write: Call out the sounds /or/, /ee/, /ie/, /oa/ and ask the students to write the letters for each one. Then call out the following words: *eel, bee, for, sort.* For each one, ask the students to listen for the sounds and write the word. Afterward, sound out each word for the students, writing the letters on the board so that they can check their work.

Further ideas
• Sing the /ee or/ song from Jolly Songs.
• Make a collage of trees in a storm.
• Make model seesaws from modeling clay.
• Pin up the /ee or/ section of the Wall Frieze.

Extra support: Remember to assess and identify any students who are struggling and provide them with the extra support they need. See pages 17 to 19 for more information.

  : 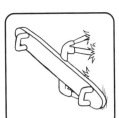  : 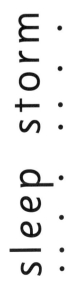 :

ee or

ee or ee or

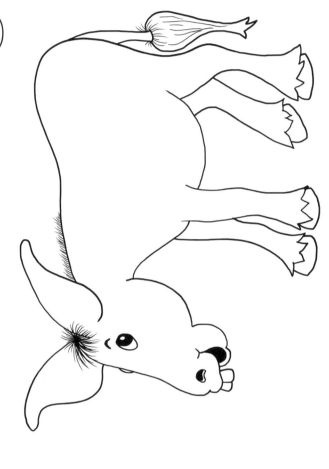

bee	corn
tree	fork
sleep	storm

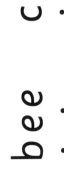 ee

 or

Letter Sound: /z/

Flashcards: Review the letter sounds already taught: /s/, /a/, /t/, /i/, /p/, /n/, /c/, /k/, /e/, /h/, /r/, /m/, /d/, /g/, /o/, /u/, /l/, /f/, /b/, /ai/, /j/, /oa/, /ie/, /ee/, /or/.

Storyline: One sunny morning, a girl is sitting outside, playing with her toy zebra. She hears a loud buzzing noise and looks around to see Bee buzzing from flower to flower. Bee is collecting pollen from the zinnias and daisies to make into honey. The girl pretends to fly like a bee, buzzing around and saying, "zzzzzz."

 Action: The students put their arms out at their sides and flap them like a bee, making a continuous /zzzzzz/ sound.

Letter formation: Explain how the letter for /z/ is written. The students form the letter in the air. Then they practice writing the letter on their sound sheets. They write over the dotted letters and then try again, using the starting dots.

Blending: Blend the words on the sound sheet with the students: *zap, buzz, fizz, unzip.* The students point to the dot underneath each sound as they say it. More words from the word bank can be written on the board for extra blending practice.

Identifying the sounds: This activity is for aural segmenting only. Look at the three small pictures on the sound sheet. Say the words and then sound them out with the students, holding up a finger for each sound: m-a-ze, z-e-b-r-a, z-i-g-z-a-g. Say the sounds again, pointing to the dots under the words. Do some more segmenting, using short words from the word bank.

Word bank: zap, zip, zit, buzz, fizz, jazz, zest, unzip, zigzag; A bee buzzes.

Sound sheet: Encourage the students to form the letters correctly and to color the pictures neatly when completing the sound sheet.

Listen and write: Call out the sounds /z/, /or/, /ee/, /ie/ and ask the students to write the letter(s) for each one. Then call out the following words: *zip, zest, zap, zit.* For each one, ask the students to listen for the sounds and write the word. Afterward, sound out each word for the students, writing the letters on the board so that they can check their work.

Further ideas
• Sing the /z/ song from Jolly Songs.
• Make a zoo with toy zebras and other animals.
• Make some bees. Paint yellow and black stripes on paper plates and add doily wings.
• Pin up the /z/ section of the Wall Frieze.

Zz

zap

buzz

fizz

unzip

Z z z z Z

Z

Letter Sound: /w/

Flashcards: Review the letter sounds already taught: /s/, /a/, /t/, /i/, /p/, /n/, /c/, /k/, /e/, /h/, /r/, /m/, /d/, /g/, /o/, /u/, /l/, /f/, /b/, /ai/, /j/, /oa/, /ie/, /ee/, /or/, /z/.

Storyline: In Aesop's fable, the west wind and the sun argue about who is the strongest. The wind says, "See that man? I'll blow so hard that his coat comes off." He blows and blows – "w, w, w, w," – but the man holds on tightly to his warm winter coat. The sun smiles and starts to shine. The man gets warmer and warmer, until he takes off his coat. "I win!" says the sun.

Action: The students cup their hands and blow on them, as if they are being the wind, saying *w, w, w, w.*

Letter formation: Explain how the letter for /w/ is written. The students form the letter in the air. Then they practice writing the letter on their sound sheets. They write over the dotted letters and then try again, using the starting dots.

Blending: Blend the words on the sound sheet with the students: *web, twig, week, wind.* The students point to the dot underneath each sound as they say it. More words from the word bank can be written on the board for extra blending practice.

Identifying the sounds: This activity is for aural segmenting only. Look at the three small pictures on the sound sheet. Say the words and then sound them out with the students, holding up a finger for each sound: s-w-i-m, w-e-ll, s-w-a-n. Say the sounds again, pointing to the dots under the words. Do some more segmenting, using short words from the word bank.

Word bank: wag, web, wet, wig, win, well, wick, will, wail, wait, weed, week, weep, worn, swam, swim, swum, twig, twin, went, wept, west, wilt, wind, swell, sweep, sweet, tweet, waist, swept, swift, twist, unwell, cobweb, wigwam, wombat, weekend, windmill, sweetcorn; flies in a web.

Sound sheet: Encourage the students to form the letters correctly and to color the pictures neatly when completing the sound sheet.

Listen and write: Call out the sounds /w/, /z/, /or/, /ee/ and ask the students to write the letter(s) for each one. Then call out the following words: *wag, win, wet, weep.* For each one, ask the students to listen for the sounds and write the word. Afterward, sound out each word for the students, writing the letters on the board so that they can check their work.

Further ideas
• Sing the /w/ song from Jolly Songs.
• Make spiderwebs with wool.
• Draw pictures of a window and the view beyond.
• Pin up the /w/ section of the Wall Frieze.

W w

web
twig
week
wind

Letter Sound: /ng/

Flashcards: Review the letter sounds already taught: /s/, /a/, /t/, /i/, /p/, /n/, /c/, /k/, /e/, /h/, /r/, /m/, /d/, /g/, /o/, /u/, /l/, /f/, /b/, /ai/, /j/, /oa/, /ie/, /ee/, /or/, /z/, /w/.

Storyline: Snake is playing games and watching television. First, he bounces a ping-pong ball with a bat and then he plays with his racing car. Then he watches a very strong man lifting weights on TV. He goes outside and pretends he is a weightlifter, too. He finds a heavy log and picks it up, grunting loudly: "ng!"

 Action: The students pretend to lift a heavy weight above their head and say *ng...*

Letter formation: The sound /ng/ is written with two letters. When two letters make one sound it is called a digraph. Remind the students how both letters are formed. The students form the letters for the digraph in the air. Then they practice writing them on their sound sheets.

Blending: Blend the words on the sound sheet with the students: *sing, long, bang, strong.* The students point to the dot underneath each sound as they say it. More words from the word bank can be written on the board for extra blending practice.

Identifying the sounds: This activity is for aural segmenting only. Look at the three small pictures on the sound sheet. Say the words and then sound them out with the students, holding up a finger for each sound: r-i-ng, k-i-ng, s-w-i-ng. Say the sounds again, pointing to the dots under the words. Do some more segmenting, using short words from the word bank.

Word bank: bang, gang, gong, hang, hung, king, long, lung, rang, ring, rung, sang, sing, song, sung, wing, zing, bring, clang, cling, clung, fling, flung, sling, sting, stung, swing, swung, seeing, oblong, sprang, spring, string, strong, buzzing, running, sitting, wedding, willing, feeling, meeting, morning, railing, soaking, weeping, jumping, landing, spelling, swelling, ding-dong, freezing, painting, ping-pong, sleeping, speeding, training, smuggling; a freezing morning.

Sound sheet: Encourage the students to form the letters correctly and to color the pictures neatly when completing the sound sheet.

Listen and write: Call out the sounds /ng/, /w/, /z/, /or/ and ask the students to write the letter(s) for each one. Then call out the following words: *hang, wing, song, lung.* For each one, ask the students to listen for the sounds and write the word. Afterward, sound out each word for the students, writing the letters on the board so that they can check their work.

Further ideas
• Sing the /ng/ song from Jolly Songs.
• Play a game of ping-pong.
• Makes pictures of things using string.
• Pin up the /ng/ section of the Wall Frieze.

ng

ng

ng ng

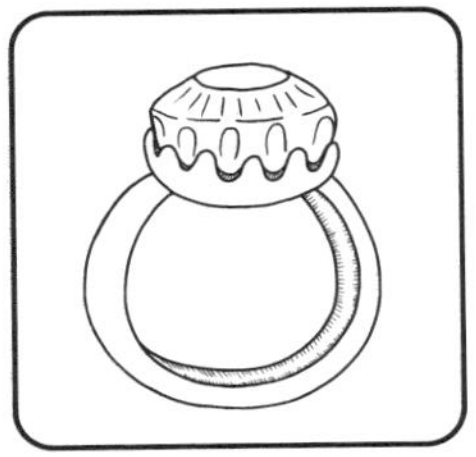

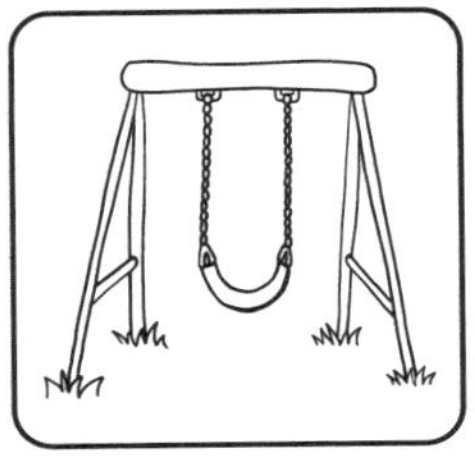

ng ng

ng ng

sing

long

bang

strong

ng

Letter Sound: /v/

Flashcards: Review the letter sounds already taught: /s/, /a/, /t/, /i/, /p/, /n/, /c/, /k/, /e/, /h/, /r/, /m/, /d/, /g/, /o/, /u/, /l/, /f/, /b/, /ai/, /j/, /oa/, /ie/, /ee/, /or/, /z/, /w/, /ng/.

Storyline: Uncle Vic is a deliveryman. He drives through the villages in his van, delivering fruit and vegetables. "Vvvvvv...VROOM," goes the van as he zooms along. Uncle Vic always waves to Inky and her friends as he is driving by. They wave back and pretend to be Uncle Vic in his van: "vvvvvv!"

 Action: The students pretend to be driving a van, turning the steering wheel and making a continuous /vvvvvv/ sound.

Letter formation: Explain how the letter for /v/ is written. The students form the letter in the air. Then they practice writing the letter on their sound sheets. They write over the dotted letters and then try again, using the starting dots.

Blending: Blend the words on the sound sheet with the students: *vet, van, vest, seven.* The students point to the dot underneath each sound as they say it. More words from the word bank can be written on the board for extra blending practice.

Identifying the sounds: This activity is for aural segmenting only. Look at the three small pictures on the sound sheet. Say the words and then sound them out with the students, holding up a finger for each sound: w-a-ve, v-a-se, f-i-ve. Say the sounds again, pointing to the dots under the words. Do some more segmenting, using short words from the word bank.

Word bank: van, vat, vet, vain, vent, vest, seven, livid, vivid, vomit, advent, invent, invest, victim; a man in a van.

Sound sheet: Encourage the students to form the letters correctly and to color the pictures neatly when completing the sound sheet.

Listen and write: Call out the sounds /v/, /ng/, /w/, /z/ and ask the students to write the letter(s) for each one. Then call out the following words: *vat, vet, van, vain.* For each one, ask the students to listen for the sounds and write the word. Afterward, sound out each word for the students, writing the letters on the board so that they can check their work.

Further ideas
• Sing the /v/ song from Jolly Songs.
• Set up a vet's surgery for toy animals.
• Wrap up parcels for Uncle Vic to deliver.
• Pin up the /v/ section of the Wall Frieze.

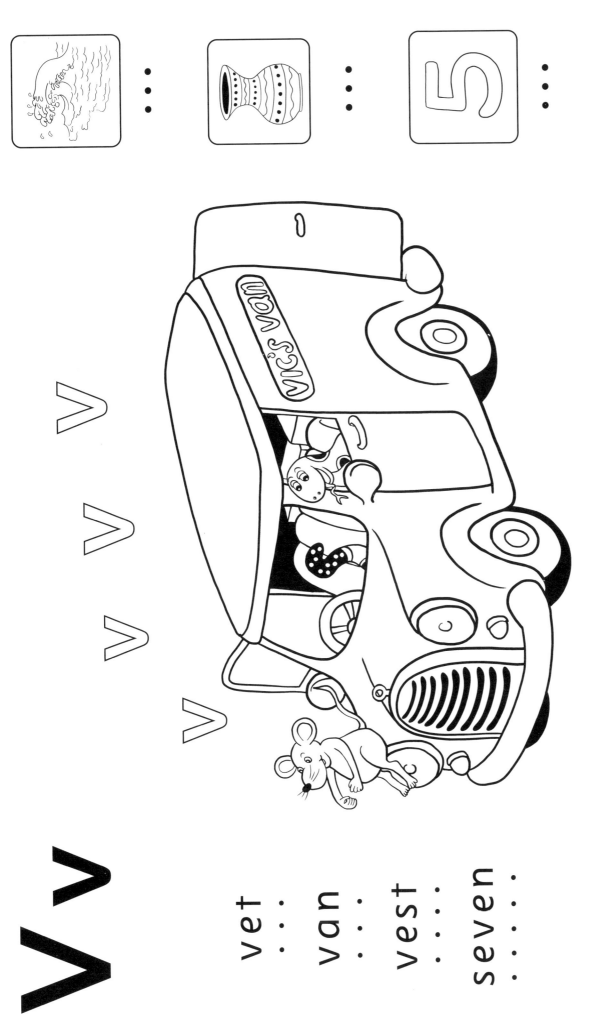

V v

v v v
v v v
v v
v v

vet : :
van : :
vest : : :
seven : : : :

Letter Sounds: /oo/ and /oo/

Flashcards: Review the letter sounds already taught: /s/, /a/, /t/, /i/, /p/, /n/, /c/, /k/, /e/, /h/, /r/, /m/, /d/, /g/, /o/, /u/, /l/, /f/, /b/, /ai/, /j/, /oa/, /ie/, /ee/, /or/, /z/, /w/, /ng/, /v/.

Storyline: A girl is visiting her great aunt, who has a big house and a large friendly cat called Noodle. It will soon be two o'clock, and the girl puts down the book she is reading and goes to wait by the old cuckoo clock. On the hour, a red, blue, and yellow cuckoo pops out from the wooden door, calling "oo-*oo*, oo-*oo*."

 Action: The students pretend to be the cuckoo in the clock, moving their heads back and forth and saying oo-*oo, oo-oo.*

Letter formation: Explain how to write the digraph ‹oo›, pointing out that one size of writing is used for both sounds. Remind the students how the two ‹o›s are formed. The students form the letters for the digraph in the air. Then they practice writing them on their sound sheets.

Blending: Blend the words on the sound sheet with the students: /oo/ *foot, look, good;* /oo/ *zoo, pool, moon.* The students point to the dot underneath each sound as they say it. More words from the word bank can be written on the board for extra blending practice. In blending words with the digraph ‹oo›, it helps to remember the saying: If one way does not work, try the other.

Identifying the sounds: This activity is for aural segmenting only. Look at the three small pictures on the sound sheet. Say the words and then sound them out with the students, holding up a finger for each sound: b-oo-k, b-oo-t, s-p-oo-n. Say the sounds again, pointing to the dots under the words. Do some more segmenting, using short words from the word bank.

Word bank:
/oo/: book, cook, foot, good, hood, hook, look, rook, soot, took, wood, woof, wool, brook, crook, stood, scrapbook, footsteps; a good cook.
/oo/: boo, moo, too, zoo, boom, boot, cool, food, hoof, hoop, hoot, loop, mood, moon, noon, pool, roof, room, root, soon, tool, toot, zoom, bloom, broom, droop, gloom, igloo, proof, roost, scoop, spook, spoon, stool, stoop, swoop, tattoo, bedroom, cloakroom, broomstick; Sit on a stool.

Sound sheet: Encourage the students to form the letters correctly and to color the pictures neatly when completing the sound sheet.

Listen and write: Call out the sounds /oo/, /oo/, /v/, /ng/ and ask the students to write the letter(s) for each one. Then call out the following words: *wood, foot, zoom, hoop.* For each one, ask the students to listen for the sounds and write the word. Afterward, sound out each word for the students, writing the letters on the board so that they can check their work.

Further ideas
• Sing the /oo oo/ song from Jolly Songs.
• Make a model cuckoo clock.
• Look at books about the moon.
• Pin up the /oo oo/ section of the Wall Frieze.

Extra support: Remember to assess and identify any students who are struggling and provide them with the extra support they need. See pages 17 to 19 for more information.

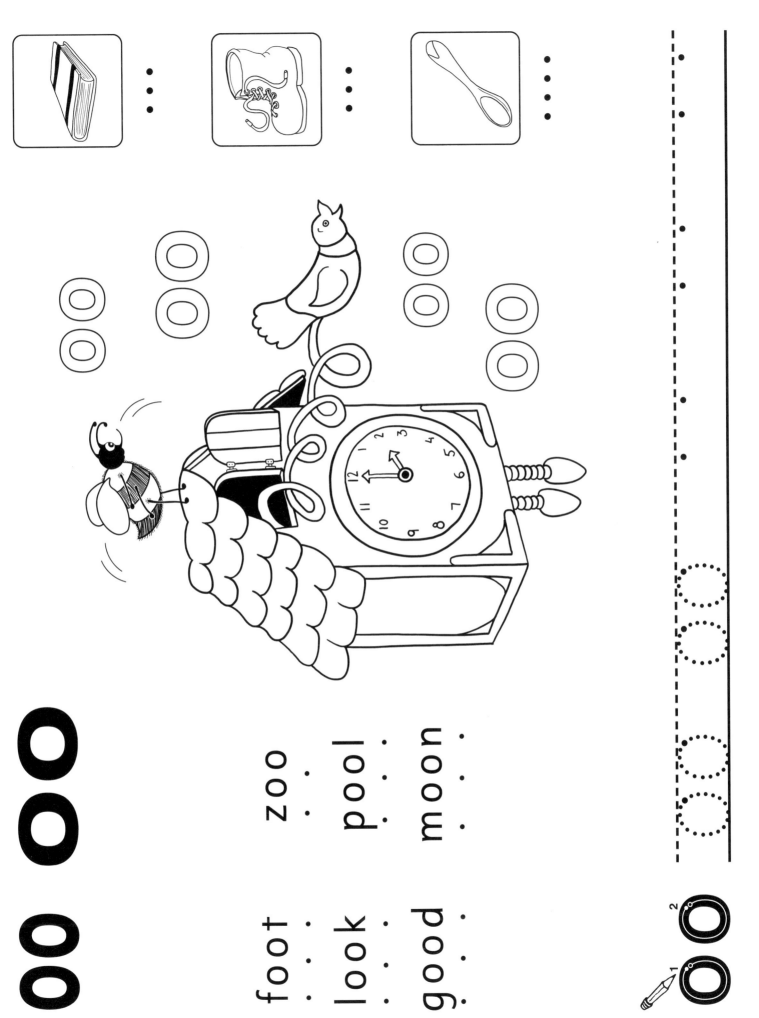

zoo

pool

moon

foot

look

good

Letter Sound: /y/

Flashcards: Review the letter sounds already taught: /s/, /a/, /t/, /i/, /p/, /n/, /c/, /k/, /e/, /h/, /r/, /m/, /d/, /g/, /o/, /u/, /l/, /f/, /b/, /ai/, /j/, /oa/, /ie/, /ee/, /or/, /z/, /w/, /ng/, /v/, /oo/, /oo/.

Storyline: It is lunchtime at school. One boy is eating his sandwich quickly so that he can play with his yo-yo. A girl is sharing a banana yogurt with her friend. She chose it yesterday when she went shopping with her dad and younger sister. "Mmm, that's nice," says the friend. "Yes, it is," says the girl. "It's a y...y...y...yummy, yellow yogurt!"

 Action: The students pretend to eat yogurt from a spoon and say *y, y, y, y.*

Letter formation: Explain how the letter for /y/ is written, pointing out that it has a tail that goes down under the line. The students form the letter in the air. Then they practice writing the letter on their sound sheets. They write over the dotted letters and then try again, using the starting dots.

Blending: Blend the words on the sound sheet with the students: *yes, yak, yell, yelp.* The students point to the dot underneath each sound as they say it. More words from the word bank can be written on the board for extra blending practice.

Identifying the sounds: This activity is for aural segmenting only. Look at the three small pictures on the sound sheet. Say the words and then sound them out with the students, holding up a finger for each sound: y-ol-k, y-a-k, y-o-y-o. Say the sounds again, pointing to the dots under the words. Do some more segmenting, using short words from the word bank.

Word bank: yak, yam, yap, yen, yes, yet, yum, yell, yuck, yelp; a big yelp.

Sound sheet: Encourage the students to form the letters correctly and to color the pictures neatly when completing the sound sheet.

Listen and write: Call out the sounds /y/, /oo/, /oo/, /v/ and ask the students to write the letter(s) for each one. Then call out the following words: *yam, yet, yum, yen.* For each one, ask the students to listen for the sounds and write the word. Afterward, sound out each word for the students, writing the letters on the board so that they can check their work.

Further ideas
• Sing the /y/ song from Jolly Songs.
• Make a yak collage using wool.
• Paint pictures of something yellow.
• Pin up the /y/ section of the Wall Frieze.

Y y

yes :
yak :
yell :
yelp :

yogurt

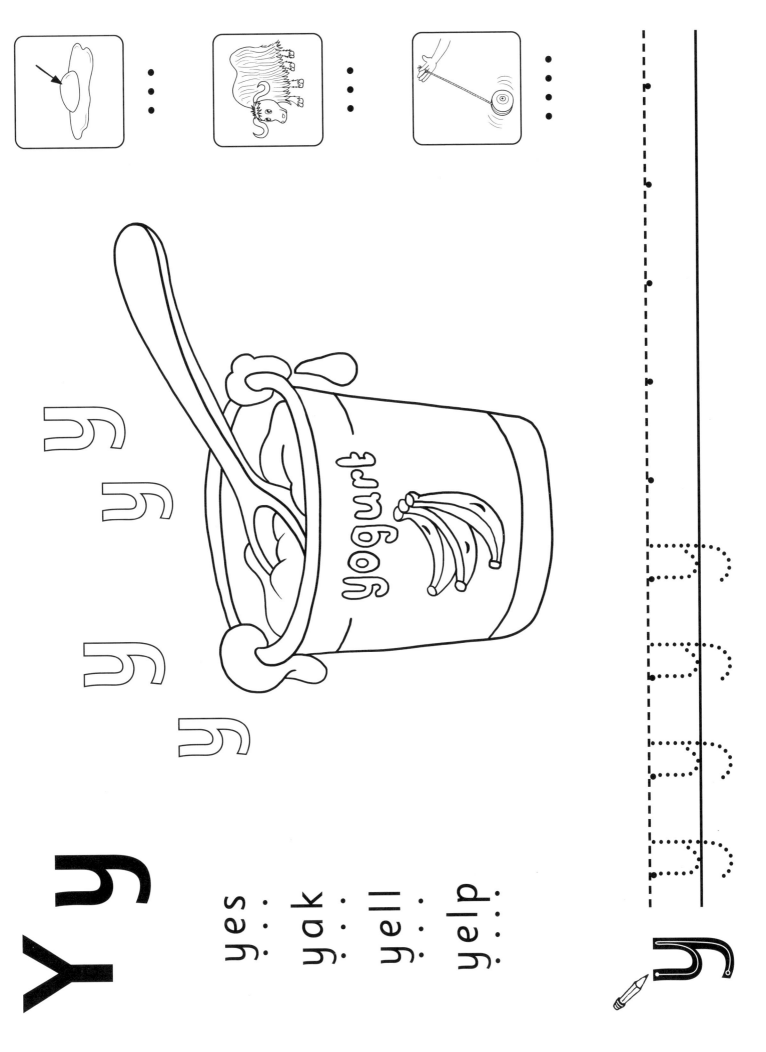

Letter Sound: /x/

Flashcards: Review the letter sounds already taught: /s/, /a/, /t/, /i/, /p/, /n/, /c/, /k/, /e/, /h/, /r/, /m/, /d/, /g/, /o/, /u/, /l/, /f/, /b/, /ai/, /j/, /oa/, /ie/, /ee/, /or/, /z/, /w/, /ng/, /v/, /oo/, /oo/, /y/.

Storyline: A boy falls out of a tree and hurts his arm. In the hospital, he has to keep it very still while some x-rays are taken: "ks, ks, ks, ks." The x-rays show that the boy's arm is broken. The nurse puts a plaster cast on the arm to stop it from moving and to help the bones mend properly.

 Action: The students pretend to take an x-ray with an x-ray camera and say *x, x, x, x.*

Letter formation: The sound /x/ is really two sounds blended together: /ks/. Explain how the letter for /x/ is written. The students form the letter in the air. Then they practice writing the letter on their sound sheets. They write over the dotted letters and then try again, using the starting dots.

Blending: Blend the words on the sound sheet with the students: *box, mix, exit, next.* The students point to the dot underneath each sound as they say it. More words from the word bank can be written on the board for extra blending practice.

Identifying the sounds: This activity is for aural segmenting only. Look at the three small pictures on the sound sheet. Say the words and then sound them out with the students, holding up a finger for each sound: f-o-x, s-i-x, t-oo-l-b-o-x. Say the sounds again, pointing to the dots under the words. Do some more segmenting, using short words from the word bank.

Word bank: ox, box, fax, fix, fox, mix, sax, six, tax, wax, coax, hoax, exit, flex, next, text, index, boxing, sixteen, toolbox, paintbox, textbook; A red fox sits in a box.

Sound sheet: Encourage the students to form the letters correctly and to color the pictures neatly when completing the sound sheet.

Listen and write: Call out the sounds /x/, /y/, /oo/, /oo/ and ask the students to write the letter(s) for each one. Then call out the following words: *fox, six, wax, next.* For each one, ask the students to listen for the sounds and write the word. Afterward, sound out each word for the students, writing the letters on the board so that they can check their work.

Further ideas
• Sing the /x/ song from Jolly Songs.
• Look at pictures of skeletons and x-rays.
• Make pictures of x-rays with white straws and black paper.
• Pin up the /x/ section of the Wall Frieze.

:

:

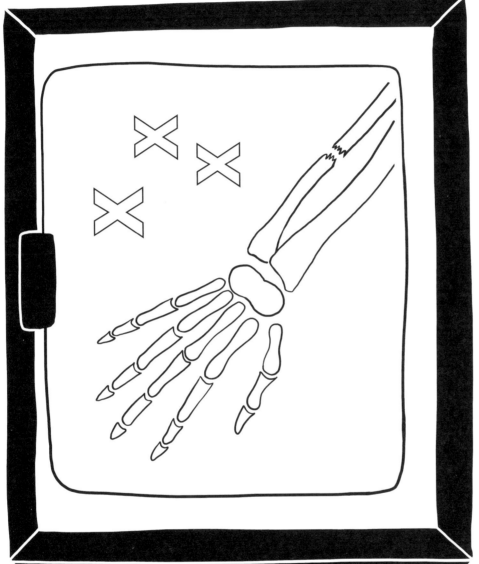

box : :
mix : :
exit : : :
next : :

Letter Sound: /ch/

Flashcards: Review the letter sounds already taught: /s/, /a/, /t/, /i/, /p/, /n/, /c/, /k/, /e/, /h/, /r/, /m/, /d/, /g/, /o/, /u/, /l/, /f/, /b/, /ai/, /j/, /oa/, /ie/, /ee/, /or/, /z/, /w/, /ng/, /v/, /oo/, /oo/, /y/, /x/.

Storyline: Some students are on a school trip. They are having a ride in an old steam train. The train starts to move off, chugging slowly: "ch, ch, ch, ch." Then it starts to go faster, chuffing loudly: "ch, ch, ch, ch!" The train gets faster and faster until steam comes out of the funnel and the whistle blows: "Choo-choo!"

 Action: The students move their arms at their sides like a steam train and say *ch, ch, ch, ch.*

Letter formation: The sound /ch/ is written with two letters. When two letters make one sound it is called a digraph. Remind the students how both letters are formed. The students form the letters for the digraph in the air. Then they practice writing them on their sound sheets.

Blending: Blend the words on the sound sheet with the students: *chop, chain, torch, bunch.* The students point to the dot underneath each sound as they say it. More words from the word bank can be written on the board for extra blending practice.

Identifying the sounds: This activity is for aural segmenting only. Look at the three small pictures on the sound sheet. Say the words and then sound them out with the students, holding up a finger for each sound: ch-i-ck, ch-e-s-t, ch-ee-se. Say the sounds again, pointing to the dots under the words. Do some more segmenting, using short words from the word bank.

Word bank: chat, chin, chip, chop, chug, inch, much, rich, such, check, chess, chick, chill, chain, cheek, coach, poach, porch, torch, bench, bunch, chest, chimp, chomp, finch, hunch, lunch, munch, pinch, punch, speech, crunch, drench, trench, screech, ostrich, cockroach, chopsticks, chimpanzee; an ostrich in a zoo.

Sound sheet: Encourage the students to form the letters correctly and to color the pictures neatly when completing the sound sheet.

Listen and write: Call out the sounds /ch/, /x/, /y/, /oo/ and ask the students to write the letter(s) for each one. Then call out the following words: *chin, chat, much, coach.* For each one, ask the students to listen for the sounds and write the word. Afterward, sound out each word for the students, writing the letters on the board so that they can check their work.

Further ideas
• Sing the /ch/ song from Jolly Songs.
• Make paper-chain decorations.
• Pretend to be a steam train. Form a line and chuff around, saying *Ch, ch, ch! Choo, choo!*
• Pin up the /ch/ section of the Wall Frieze.

ch

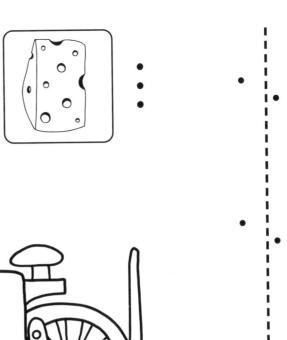
· · ·

· · ·

· · ·

chop ·
chain ·
torch ·
bunch ·

ch

Letter Sound: /sh/

Flashcards: Review the letter sounds already taught: /s/, /a/, /t/, /i/, /p/, /n/, /c/, /k/, /e/, /h/, /r/, /m/, /d/, /g/, /o/, /u/, /l/, /f/, /b/, /ai/, /j/, /oa/, /ie/, /ee/, /or/, /z/, /w/, /ng/, /v/, /oo/, /oo/, /y/, /x/, /ch/.

Storyline: Mom is trying to get the babies to sleep. She gives them their bottles and in a short while they all shut their eyes, apart from one who starts to cry. "Shshshsh," Mom whispers, rocking the baby gently. "Hush now. Don't wake up your brothers and sisters."

 Action: The students place their index finger against their lips and make a continuous /shshshsh/ sound.

Letter formation: The sound /sh/ is written with two letters. When two letters make one sound it is called a digraph. Remind the students how both letters are formed. The students form the letters for the digraph in the air. Then they practice writing them on their sound sheets.

Blending: Blend the words on the sound sheet with the students: *dish, shop, sheep, brush*. The students point to the dot underneath each sound as they say it. More words from the word bank can be written on the board for extra blending practice.

Identifying the sounds: This activity is for aural segmenting only. Look at the three small pictures on the sound sheet. Say the words and then sound them out with the students, holding up a finger for each sound: f-i-sh, sh-e-ll, sh-ar-k. Say the sounds again, pointing to the dots under the words. Do some more segmenting, using short words from the word bank.

Word bank: ash, bash, cash, dash, dish, fish, hush, mash, posh, rash, rush, shed, shin, ship, shop, shot, shut, wish, shall, shell, shock, sheep, sheet, shook, shoot, short, blush, brush, crash, crush, flash, flush, fresh, shelf, shift, shred, shrug, slush, smash, shrill, finish, polish, punish, shrimp, splash, vanish, eggshell, shampoo, shopping, selfish, shellfish, mushroom, paintbrush; sixteen books on a shelf.

Sound sheet: Encourage the students to form the letters correctly and to color the pictures neatly when completing the sound sheet.

Listen and write: Call out the sounds /sh/, /ch/, /x/, /y/ and ask the students to write the letter(s) for each one. Then call out the following words: *rash, shed, wish, sheet*. For each one, ask the students to listen for the sounds and write the word. Afterward, sound out each word for the students, writing the letters on the board so that they can check their work.

Tricky words: Introduce the tricky word *I*. Explain that this word is tricky because it uses its letter name and not its sound. We say it is very shy, so it puffs itself up into its capital letter. Underline the word in purple on the board to show the tricky part. Pin up the Tricky Word Wall Flower for *I*.

Further ideas
• Sing the /sh/ song from Jolly Songs.
• Make sheep with cotton ball fleeces.
• Make a shaker with two yogurt pots and some uncooked rice.
• Pin up the /sh/ section of the Wall Frieze.

  :   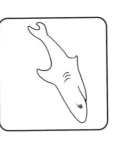 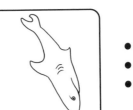 : :

sh

sh sh sh

sh

dish

shop

sheep

brush

sh

Letter Sounds: /th/ and /th/

Flashcards: Review the tricky word *I* and the letter sounds already taught: /s/, /a/, /t/, /i/, /p/, /n/, /c/, /k/, /e/, /h/, /r/, /m/, /d/, /g/, /o/, /u/, /l/, /f/, /b/, /ai/, /j/, /oa/, /ie/, /ee/, /or/, /z/, /w/, /ng/, /v/, /oo/, /oo/, /y/, /x/, /ch/, /sh/.

Storyline: The clowns at the circus are very funny. They run around the ring, throwing water at the ringmaster, and then tickle each other with feathers. One naughty clown is rather rude. He sticks the tip of his tongue out and says, "th!" Another clown is very rude. He sticks his tongue right out, saying, "thththth."

 Action: The students act like rude clowns, sticking out their tongues a little for /th/ and further for /th/.

Letter formation: Explain how to write the digraph ‹th›, pointing out that one size of writing is used for both sounds. Remind the students how both letters are formed. The students form the letters for the digraph in the air. Then they practice writing them on their sound sheets.

Blending: Blend the words on the sound sheet with the students: /th/ *this, that, then;* /th/ *thin, moth, three*. The students point to the dot underneath each sound as they say it. More words from the word bank can be written on the board for extra blending practice. In blending words with the digraph ‹th›, it helps to remember the saying: If one way does not work, try the other.

Identifying the sounds: This activity is for aural segmenting only. Look at the three small pictures on the sound sheet. Say the words and then sound them out with the students, holding up a finger for each sound: th-u-mb, f-ea-th-er, t-oo-th. Say the sounds again, pointing to the dots under the words. Do some more segmenting, using short words from the word bank.

Word bank:
/th/: than, that, them, then, this, with, smooth, within; a goat with big horns.
/th/: moth, thin, thud, thick, faith, north, teeth, thing, thorn, three, tooth, broth, cloth, froth, sixth, tenth, theft, throb, thump, thrill, length, throat, thrush, strength, toothbrush; thick socks for boots.

Sound sheet: Encourage the students to form the letters correctly and to color the pictures neatly when completing the sound sheet.

Listen and write: Call out the sounds /th/, /th/, /sh/, /ch/ and ask the students to write the letters for each one. Then call out the following words: *than, with, tooth, thud*. For each one, ask the students to listen for the sounds and write the word. Afterward, sound out each word for the students, writing the letters on the board so that they can check their work.

Tricky words: Introduce the tricky word *the*. This word is tricky because although the ‹th› is written as it sounds, the students must remember to write an ‹e› on the end. Work out the tricky part together and underline it in purple on the board. Pin up the Tricky Word Wall Flower for *the*.

Further ideas
• Sing the /th th/ song from Jolly Songs.
• Make pictures decorated with feathers.
• Find out about different types of moths.
• Pin up the /th th/ section of the Wall Frieze.

Extra support: Remember to assess and identify any students who are struggling and provide them with the extra support they need. See pages 17 to 19 for more information.

th

th th

th th

thin

this

that moth

then three

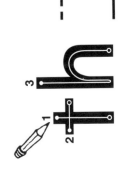

Letter Sound: /qu/

Flashcards: Review the tricky words *I, the* and the letter sounds already taught: /s/, /a/, /t/, /i/, /p/, /n/, /c/, /k/, /e/, /h/, /r/, /m/, /d/, /g/, /o/, /u/, /l/, /f/, /b/, /ai/, /j/, /oa/, /ie/, /ee/, /or/, /z/, /w/, /ng/, /v/, /oo/, /oo/, /y/, /x/, /ch/, /sh/, /th/, /th/.

Storyline: At the park a boy is feeding some stale bread to the ducks and squirrels. The squirrels scamper over quickly and quietly. Two of them grab the same slice and begin to quarrel, squeaking at each other. The ducks rush to the side of the pond, quacking loudly. The boy laughs and pretends to be a duck too, saying, "qu, qu, qu, qu."

 Action: The students open and close their hands like a duck's beak and say *qu, qu, qu, qu.*

Letter formation: The sound /qu/ is really two sounds blended together: /kw/. Explain how to write the digraph ‹qu›, pointing out that ‹q› starts with a caterpillar /c/ and has a tail that goes under the line. It is never used on its own in English words. The students form the letters for the digraph in the air. Then they practice writing them on their sound sheets.

Blending: Blend the words on the sound sheet with the students: *quiz, squid, quack, squirrel.* The students point to the dot underneath each sound as they say it. More words from the word bank can be written on the board for extra blending practice.

Identifying the sounds: This activity is for aural segmenting only. Look at the three small pictures on the sound sheet. Say the words and then sound them out with the students, holding up a finger for each sound: qu-ee-n, qu-i-l-t, s-q-ui-d. Say the sounds again, pointing to the dots under the words. Do some more segmenting, using short words from the word bank.

Word bank: quin, quit, quiz, quack, quick, quill, quail queen, quench, quest, quilt, squid, liquid, squint, quacking, quicksand; three quacking ducks; She will win the quiz.

Sound sheet: Encourage the students to form the letters correctly and to color the pictures neatly when completing the sound sheet.

Listen and write: Call out the sounds /qu/, /th/, /th/, /sh/ and ask the students to write the letters for each one. Then call out the following words: *quit, quail, quin, quest.* For each one, ask the students to listen for the sounds and write the word. Afterward, sound out each word for the students, writing the letters on the board so that they can check their work.

Tricky words: Introduce the tricky words *he* and *she*. These words are tricky because although the ‹h› and ‹sh› are written as they sound, the sound /ee/ in both words is written with only one ‹e›. Together, work out the tricky part in each word and underline it in purple on the board. Pin up the Tricky Word Wall Flowers for *he* and *she*.

Further ideas
• Sing the /qu/ song from Jolly Songs.
• Paint pictures of quacking ducks on a pond.
• Make a squirrel collage, using wool for the tails.
• Pin up the /qu/ section of the Wall Frieze.

Qu qu nb

qu nb

qu nb

qu nb

quiz

squid

quack

squirrel

Letter Sound: /ou/

Flashcards: Review the tricky words *I, the, he, she* and the letter sounds already taught: /s/, /a/, /t/, /i/, /p/, /n/, /c/, /k/, /e/, /h/, /r/, /m/, /d/, /g/, /o/, /u/, /l/, /f/, /b/, /ai/, /j/, /oa/, /ie/, /ee/, /or/, /z/, /w/, /ng/, /v/, /oo/, /oo/, /y/, /x/, /ch/, /sh/, /th/, /th/, /qu/.

Storyline: At Granny's house, a girl is learning how to sew. She wants to make a mat with a brown owl on it. They sit down on the couch and get out the sewing basket. Granny threads two needles, one with brown thread and the other with black. Suddenly, the girl frowns and shouts, "ou!" She has pricked her thumb with the needle!"

Action: The students pretend that their finger is a needle and use it to prick their thumb, saying *ou!*

Letter formation: The sound /ou/ is written with two letters. When two letters make one sound it is called a digraph. Remind the students how both letters are formed. The students form the letters for the digraph in the air. Then they practice writing them on their sound sheets.

Blending: Blend the words on the sound sheet with the students: *out, loud, shout, mouth.* The students point to the dot underneath each sound as they say it. More words from the word bank can be written on the board for extra blending practice.

Identifying the sounds: This activity is for aural segmenting only. Look at the three small pictures on the sound sheet. Say the words and then sound them out with the students, holding up a finger for each sound: m-ou-se, c-l-ou-d, h-ou-se. Say the sounds again, pointing to the dots under the words. Do some more segmenting, using short words from the word bank.

Word bank: out, ouch, loud, noun, couch, mouth, pouch, shout, south, cloud, count, found, hound, joust, pound, proud, round, scout, snout, sound, spout, stout, trout, wound, crouch, outing, slouch, ground, outfit, sprout, without, background; big black rain clouds; We found the missing ring.

Sound sheet: Encourage the students to form the letters correctly and to color the pictures neatly when completing the sound sheet.

Listen and write: Call out the sounds /ou/, /qu/, /th/, /th/ and ask the students to write the letters for each one. Then call out the following words: *south, couch, found, joust.* For each one, ask the students to listen for the sounds and write the word. Afterward, sound out each word for the students, writing the letters on the board so that they can check their work.

Tricky words: Introduce the tricky words *me* and *we*. These words are tricky because although the ‹m› and ‹w› are written as they sound, the sound /ee/ in both words is written with only one ‹e›. Together, work out the tricky part in each word and underline it in purple on the board. Pin up the Tricky Word Wall Flowers for *me* and *we*.

Further ideas
• Sing the /ou/ song from Jolly Songs.
• Make pictures of houses, using card and colored laces.
• Make mobiles with cut-out clouds decorated with cotton balls or black paint.
• Pin up the /ou/ section of the Wall Frieze.

ou

ou   ou

ou   ou

ou

out · loud · shout · mouth ·

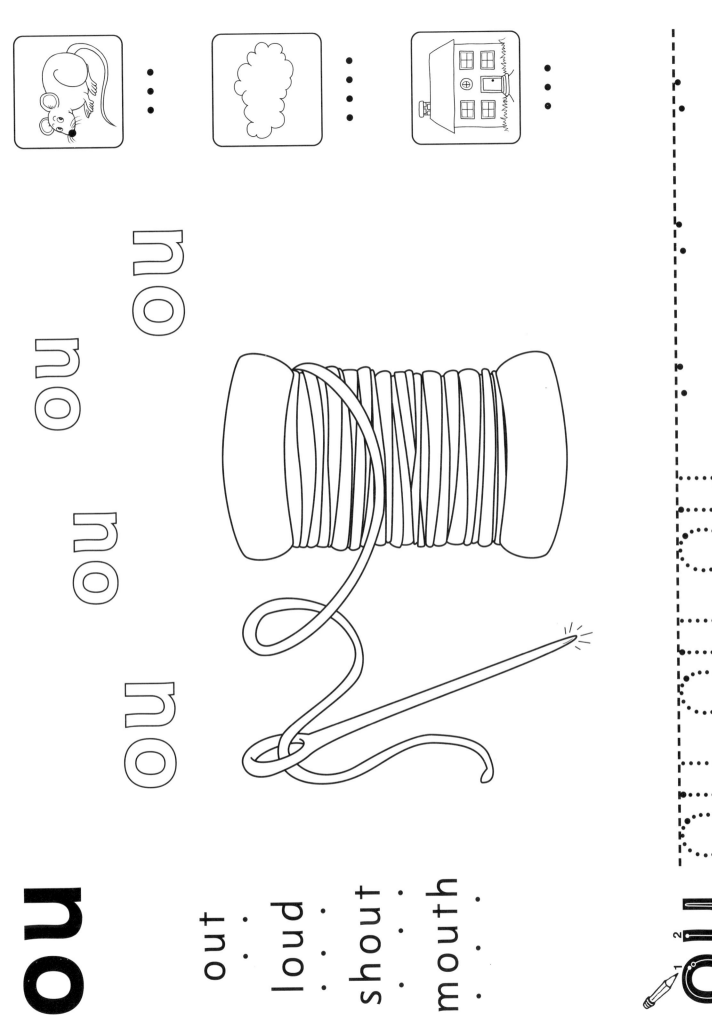

Letter Sound: /oi/

Flashcards: Review the tricky words *I, the, he, she, me, we* and the letter sounds already taught: /s/, /a/, /t/, /i/, /p/, /n/, /c/, /k/, /e/, /h/, /r/, /m/, /d/, /g/, /o/, /u/, /l/, /f/, /b/, /ai/, /j/, /oa/, /ie/, /ee/, /or/, /z/, /w/, /ng/, /v/, /oo/, /oo/, /y/, /x/, /ch/, /sh/, /th/, /th/, /qu/, /ou/.

Storyline: Inky and Snake are out in a boat called Sailor Boy. They are really enjoying themselves when BANG! There is a loud noise as the boat hits an oil drum in the water. "Look!" says Inky, pointing, "It's made a hole." They see a ship nearby and call for help: "Oi! Ship ahoy!" The sailors hear them and help them get Sailor Boy back to shore.

 Action: The students cup their hands around their mouth, as if they are hailing a passing boat, and say *oi, ship ahoy!*

Letter formation: The sound /oi/ is written with two letters. When two letters make one sound it is called a digraph. Remind the students how both letters are formed. The students form the letters for the digraph in the air. Then they practice writing them on their sound sheets.

Blending: Blend the words on the sound sheet with the students: *oil, join, soil, point.* The students point to the dot underneath each sound as they say it. More words from the word bank can be written on the board for extra blending practice.

Identifying the sounds: This activity is for aural segmenting only. Look at the three small pictures on the sound sheet. Say the words and then sound them out with the students, holding up a finger for each sound: c-oi-n, b-oi-l, t-oi-l-e-t. Say the sounds again, pointing to the dots under the words. Do some more segmenting, using short words from the word bank.

Word bank: oil, boil, coil, coin, foil, join, soil, toil, void, joint, moist, point, spoil, oilcan, tinfoil, topsoil, boiling, spoilsport; boiling oil; He will be joining us.

Sound sheet: Encourage the students to form the letters correctly and to color the pictures neatly when completing the sound sheet.

Listen and write: Call out the sounds /oi/, /ou/, /qu/, /th/ and ask the students to write the letters for each one. Then call out the following words: *toil, moist, foil, joint.* For each one, ask the students to listen for the sounds and write the word. Afterward, sound out each word for the students, writing the letters on the board so that they can check their work.

Tricky words: Introduce the tricky word *be.* This word is tricky because although the ‹b› is written as it sounds, the sound /ee/ is written with only one ‹e›. Work out the tricky part together and underline it in purple on the board. Pin up the Tricky Word Wall Flower for *be.*

Further ideas
• Sing the /oi/ song from Jolly Songs.
• Make boats from tinfoil.
• Do coin rubbings with paper and crayons.
• Pin up the /oi/ section of the Wall Frieze.

oi

oi

oi

oi

oil

join

soil

point

Letter Sound: /ue/

Flashcards: Review the tricky words *I, the, he, she, me, we, be* and the letter sounds already taught: /s/, /a/, /t/, /i/, /p/, /n/, /c/, /k/, /e/, /h/, /r/, /m/, /d/, /g/, /o/, /u/, /l/, /f/, /b/, /ai/, /j/, /oa/, /ie/, /ee/, /or/, /z/, /w/, /ng/, /v/, /oo/, /oo/, /y/, /x/, /ch/, /sh/, /th/, /th/, /qu/, /ou/, /oi/.

Storyline: The creepy crawlies are having a party and Inky is doing some magic tricks. She has a huge magic box with a unicorn on the side. She points to one of the spiders and says, "You! Will you come and help me?" The spider waves the magic wand and says, "ue, ue, ue, ue." Right on cue, a rabbit appears!

 Action: The students point to each other, saying *ue, ue, ue, ue.*

Letter formation: The sound /ue/ is written with two letters. When two letters make one sound it is called a digraph. Remind the students how both letters are formed. The students form the letters for the digraph in the air. Then they practice writing them on their sound sheets. The sound /ue/ is really two sounds blended together: /yoo/.

Blending: Blend the words on the sound sheet with the students: *fuel, value, statue, rescue.* The students point to the dot underneath each sound as they say it. More words from the word bank can be written on the board for extra blending practice. In words like *blue* and *glue*, the ‹ue› says the long /oo/ sound. In blending, it helps to remember the saying: If one way does not work, try the other.

Identifying the sounds: This activity is for aural segmenting only. Look at the three small pictures on the sound sheet. Say the words and then sound them out with the students, holding up a finger for each sound: m-e-n-u, e-m-u, p-er-f-u-me. Say the sounds again, pointing to the dots under the words. Do some more segmenting, using short words from the word bank.

Word bank: cue, hue, fuel, value, rescue, statue; a quick rescue; The fuel was good value.

Sound sheet: Encourage the students to form the letters correctly and to color the pictures neatly when completing the sound sheet.

Listen and write: Call out the sounds /ue/, /oi/, /ou/, /qu/ and ask the students to write the letters for each one. Then call out the following words: *cue, fuel, value, statue.* For each one, ask the students to listen for the sounds and write the word. Afterward, sound out each word for the students, writing the letters on the board so that they can check their work.

Tricky words: Introduce the tricky word *was*. This word is tricky because the ‹as› says /oz/. To help remember the spelling, say it as it sounds, pronouncing *was* to rhyme with *mass*. Work out the tricky part together and underline it in purple on the board. Pin up the Tricky Word Wall Flower for *was*.

Further ideas
• Sing the /ue/ song from Jolly Songs.
• Draw pictures of a rescue.
• Make small statues from modeling clay.
• Pin up the /ue/ section of the Wall Frieze.

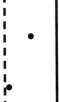

ue

ue ue

ue ue

fuel · : ·
value · : · ·
statue · : · · ·
rescue · : · · ·

 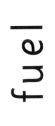

u e

Letter Sound: /er/

Flashcards: Review the tricky words *I, the, he, she, me, we, be, was* and the letter sounds already taught: /s/, /a/, /t/, /i/, /p/, /n/, /c/, /k/, /e/, /h/, /r/, /m/, /d/, /g/, /o/, /u/, /l/, /f/, /b/, /ai/, /j/, /oa/, /ie/, /ee/, /or/, /z/, /w/, /ng/, /v/, /oo/, /oo/, /y/, /x/, /ch/, /sh/, /th/, /th/, /qu/, /ou/, /oi/, /ue/.

Storyline: A brother and sister are making gingerbread for supper. They weigh the butter, sugar, ginger, eggs, and flour, and stir them together in a bowl: "er-er-er-er," goes the mixer. When the mixture is ready, they make gingerbread boys and girls and bake them in the oven.

 Action: The students roll their hands over each other like a mixer and say *er-er-er-er*.

Letter formation: The sound /er/ is written with two letters. When two letters make one sound it is called a digraph. Remind the students how both letters are formed. The students form the letters for the digraph in the air. Then they practice writing them on their sound sheets.

Blending: Blend the words on the sound sheet with the students: *letter, number, winter, summer*. The students point to the dot underneath each sound as they say it. More words from the word bank can be written on the board for extra blending practice.

Identifying the sounds: This activity is for aural segmenting only. Look at the three small pictures on the sound sheet. Say the words and then sound them out with the students, holding up a finger for each sound: h-a-mm-er, s-p-i-d-er, l-a-dd-er. Say the sounds again, pointing to the dots under the words. Do some more segmenting, using short words from the word bank.

Word bank: her, fern, herd, jerk, perm, term, verb, perch, mixer, butter, dinner, hammer, ladder, letter, litter, pepper, stern, summer, corner, deeper, singer, waiter, chatter, duster, expert, jester, number, silver, sister, winter, mermaid, blender, monster, printer, helicopter, understand, thunderstorm; a big bad monster; I will do the dinner; Her sister sent a letter to me.

Sound sheet: Encourage the students to form the letters correctly and to color the pictures neatly when completing the sound sheet.

Listen and write: Call out the sounds /er/, /ue/, /oi/, /ou/ and ask the students to write the letters for each one. Then call out the following words: *her, fern, sister, waiter*. For each one, ask the students to listen for the sounds and write the word. Afterward, sound out each word for the students, writing the letters on the board so that they can check their work.

Tricky words: Introduce the tricky words *to* and *do*. These words are tricky because although the ‹t› and ‹d› are written as they sound, the long /oo/ in both words is written with only one ‹o›. Together, work out the tricky part in each word and underline it in purple on the board. Pin up the Tricky Word Wall Flowers for *to* and *do*.

Further ideas
- Sing the /er/ song from Jolly Songs.
- Make summer and winter collages.
- Make gingerbread-family mobiles, cut out of paper or card and decorated.
- Pin up the /er/ section of the Wall Frieze.

er

er _er_ _er_ _er_ _er_ _er_

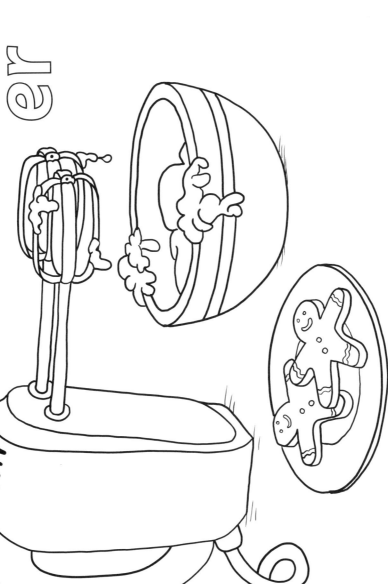

letter : . . .
number : . . .
winter : . . .
summer : . . .

Letter Sound: /ar/

Flashcards: Review the tricky words *I, the, he, she, me, we, be, was, to, do* and the letter sounds already taught: /s/, /a/, /t/, /i/, /p/, /n/, /c/, /k/, /e/, /h/, /r/, /m/, /d/, /g/, /o/, /u/, /l/, /f/, /b/, /ai/, /j/, /oa/, /ie/, /ee/, /or/, /z/, /w/, /ng/, /v/, /oo/, /oo/, /y/, /x/, /ch/, /sh/, /th/, /th/, /qu/, /ou/, /oi/, /ue/, /er/.

Storyline: : A family is on vacation by the ocean. So far, they have seen the sharks in the aquarium and bought some postcards in the market. Now they are in the harbor, looking at starfish. Suddenly, they hear a loud noise. Over on the rocks is a big brown seal. He is flapping his flippers and barking loudly, "ar, ar, ar, ar."

 Action: The students pretend to be a seal, clapping their hands loosely and saying *ar, ar, ar, ar.*

Letter formation: The sound /ar/ is written with two letters. When two letters make one sound it is called a digraph. Remind the students how both letters are formed. The students form the letters for the digraph in the air. Then they practice writing them on their sound sheets.

Blending: Blend the words on the sound sheet with the students: *jar, dark, shark, farmer.* The students point to the dot underneath each sound as they say it. More words from the word bank can be written on the board for extra blending practice.

Identifying the sounds: This activity is for aural segmenting only. Look at the three small pictures on the sound sheet. Say the words and then sound them out with the students, holding up a finger for each sound: s-t-ar, c-ar, s-c-ar-f. Say the sounds again, pointing to the dots under the words. Do some more segmenting, using short words from the word bank.

Word bank: ark, arm, art, bar, car, far, jar, tar, arch, bark, barn, card, cart, dark, dart, farm, hard, harm, harp, mark, park, part, scar, star, tart, yard, argue, charm, chart, harsh, march, marsh, shark, sharp, scarf, smart, spark, start, barber, farmer, larder, sharper, artist, cartoon, darling, garlic, partner, darkroom, farmyard, starfish, starling; ten sharks with sharp teeth; All the coins are in a jar; The sheep are in the barn.

Sound sheet: Encourage the students to form the letters correctly and to color the pictures neatly when completing the sound sheet.

Listen and write: Call out the sounds /ar/, /er/, /ue/, /oi/ and ask the students to write the letters for each one. Then call out the following words: *arch, barn, yard, smart.* For each one, ask the students to listen for the sounds and write the word. Afterward, sound out each word for the students, writing the letters on the board so that they can check their work.

Tricky words: Introduce the tricky words *are* and *all*. The word *are* is tricky because the ‹e› on the end is silent. The word *all* is tricky because the sound /o/ is written using the alternative spelling ‹al›. Together, work out the tricky part in each word and underline it in purple on the board. Once the students know the word *all*, they can read words like *ball, call, fall, hall, and tall.* Pin up the Tricky Word Wall Flowers for *are* and *all*.

Further ideas
- Sing the /ar/ song from Jolly Songs.
- Decorate jars or cards with stars.
- Find out about different types of sharks.
- Pin up the /ar/ section of the Wall Frieze.

Extra support: Remember to assess and identify any students who are struggling and provide them with the extra support they need. See pages 17 to 19 for more information.

ar

 :  :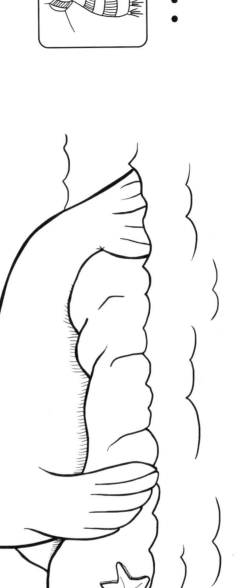

ar ar ar

ar ar

jar · · ·
dark · · ·
shark · · ·
farmer · · ·

ar

Flashcard Sheets

Once the students have been taught a letter sound, it needs to be reviewed regularly, along with the other letter sounds already taught, using flashcards. As soon as the students see the letter or digraph on the flashcard, they should be able to call out the sound and do the action. The actions keep the students engaged, but it helps occasionally to encourage them to leave out the action and say the sound only once, as this promotes the skill of blending.

The following flashcard sheets can be copied, pasted onto card, and cut up into individual flashcards. The letter sounds are grouped in their recommended teaching order.

As the students are introduced to the alternative spellings in Steps 2 and 3, the flashcards in Reproducible Section 11 can be used (see pages 188 to 191). The flashcard for ‹ck› is in this section.

s

a

t

i

p

n

ck

e

h

r

m

d

g

o

u

l

f

b

ai

j

oa

ie

ee

or

z

w

ng

v

oo

oo

y

x

ch

sh

th

th

qu ou

oi ue

er ar

Sound Book Sheets

While the students learn the letter sounds, it is a good idea for them to have their own individual sound book. This is a small book containing the letter sounds taught so far. The students take it home every day and practice the letter sounds for homework. It is also important to go through the book regularly with each student at school to see how well they are getting on. Visual rewards, such as stars stuck on the cover, provide much encouragement to parents and students alike and stimulate further interest and improvement.

The sound book sheets on the following pages can be copied, cut up into individual sounds, and pasted into each student's sound book at the appropriate time. The letter sounds are grouped in their recommended teaching order.

The sheets can also be made into letter-sound cards, which can be used in a variety of ways both at home and at school. Two copies of each sheet can be given to parents (either as the work progresses or at an initial parents' meeting), along with instructions on how to play some simple games and activities, which will help their child to practice the letter sounds.

Dear Parent,

As each group of letter sounds is taught, your child will bring home two copies of a sheet with the letters on it. Please paste the sheets onto card and cut them up into letter sounds, ready for these games and activities:

1. The pairs game

This is very useful for developing memory and reasoning, as well as for learning the letter sounds. To play, the letters are placed face down. Each player takes turns to turn over two cards, saying the sound on each card. If the sounds are the same, the player keeps the cards and has another turn. If not, the cards are turned back over and the next player has a turn. The player to get the most pairs is the winner.

2. Reading words

Arrange the letters to make simple regular words like *ant* or *tin*. Your child has to blend the sounds together to read the word.

3. Building words

Say a simple regular word. Your child has to listen for the sounds, pick up the letters that make those sounds, and lay them in the correct order. Then (s)he can check whether the word is correct by blending the sounds to read the word. In the beginning some help is needed, but gradually your child will be able to do this without assistance.

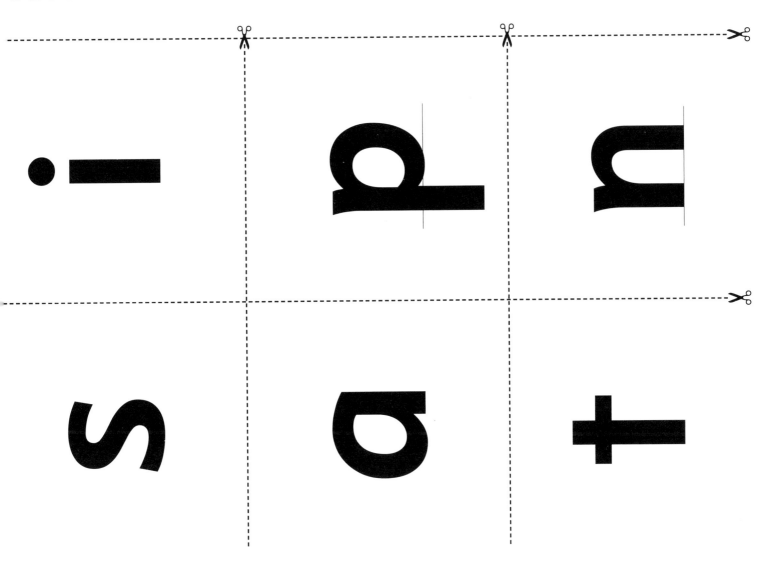

l

f

b

g

o

u

r

m

d

ck

e

h

v

oo

oo

z

w

ng

ie

ee

or

ai

j

oa

ae ue

er

ar

qu u↑

ou

oi

sh

th u

th

y

x

ch

Word Box Sheets

Blending is one of the essential skills for reading and needs to be taught from the beginning. Each lesson should provide plenty of blending practice for the students, and blending words are available on the sound sheets and in the word banks in the lesson plans. However, there is still a need for individual blending practice and this can be done at home, with a parent's help, using word boxes. Going through the word boxes is an important step as it helps the students achieve greater fluency before they are given decodable books to read for themselves.

The following word box sheets provide groups of regular blending words that have been carefully graded, progressing from very simple words, using the earliest learned letter sounds, to more complex multisyllabic words. After the fifth group of letter sounds has been taught, the word boxes can start being taken home. Once the students have reached this stage, they are eager to practice their skills and, if there is parental help, the students progress through this stage more quickly. Most students can manage a new group of words every night.

The word boxes provide the stepping stones between recognizing letters, blending words, and reading books, and care should be taken to introduce them only when the students are able to hear words that they have blended by themselves. In this way, a sense of achievement is experienced by all the students. Inevitably, the students with good visual memories will be able to read some words without saying the sounds. This is to be encouraged but should not be demanded. The aim here is to develop the skill of working out the words, rather than developing visual memory.

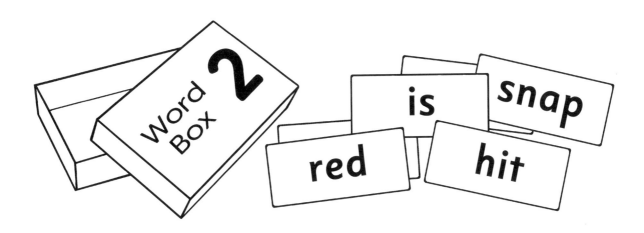

Word Box 1	Word Box 2	Word Box 3
it	pest	hip
tin	tap	pet
pat	pin	mat
nip	is	ran
sat	pit	dip
as	snap	hand
ant	in	map
tip	man	rat
pan	red	his
sit	hit	rip

Word Box 4	Word Box 5	Word Box 6
cat	kiss	drip
hen	mist	miss
can	best	rock
hat	hiss	back
neck	test	duck
camp	get	pot
kick	puff	gas
met	log	fit
pen	fat	stamp
deck	bat	bad

Word Box 7	Word Box 8	Word Box 9
leg	mud	bit
rot	from	let
up	grill	tub
top	spot	lick
but	lap	sniff
flag	mom	soft
brick	fan	frog
slip	flat	luck
fog	lamp	cup
flap	dad	not

Word Box 10	Word Box 11	Word Box 12
paint	keep	wet
jet	sleep	zip
rain	die	swim
jug	for	buzz
boat	fork	ring
pie	green	long
bee	torch	van
goat	tail	look
nail	road	cling
soap	weed	swing

Word Box 13	Word Box 14	Word Box 15
bang	yes	box
string	six	that
fizz	fox	with
good	chip	thin
zoo	chick	moth
roof	shed	thank
swam	flash	rich
tooth	wish	shut
wool	chest	ship
strong	shock	think

Word Box 16	Word Box 17	Word Box 18
yet	loud	quick
shelf	quit	out
lunch	butter	shout
crash	bark	queen
brush	soil	boil
thick	hotter	oil
shell	found	due
sink	start	park
rash	charm	shark
fish	point	litter

Matching Letters, Words, and Pictures

The following sheets group the letter sounds in the order they are taught, together with a word and picture for each letter sound. The cards for ‹k› are on page 193 in Reproducible Section 11. They can be copied, pasted onto card, and cut up into letter sound, word, and picture cards. These cards can be used in several ways to help the students learn to read and write. For example:

1. a. Lay the first group of picture and letter-sound cards out, and ask the students to look at each picture in turn and listen for the initial sound in the word. If they can hear the sound, the students look for the appropriate letter and put it under the picture.
   b. The same activity can be done in reverse by asking the students to look at a letter and say its sound. They then find the picture that shows a word starting with that sound. After the first three sheets, the initial letter is not always applicable and the students may have to listen for a medial or final sound.
   c. Later the word cards can be used in a similar way: the students blend the sounds together to read a word and put the appropriate picture underneath, or they look at the picture card first and find the word to match.

2. Pairs Games: match either the letters or the words to the pictures (see the parents' instructions on page 113 for how to play).

s	sun	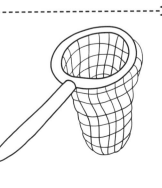
a	ant	
t	ten	
i	ink	
p	pan	
n	net	

c	cup	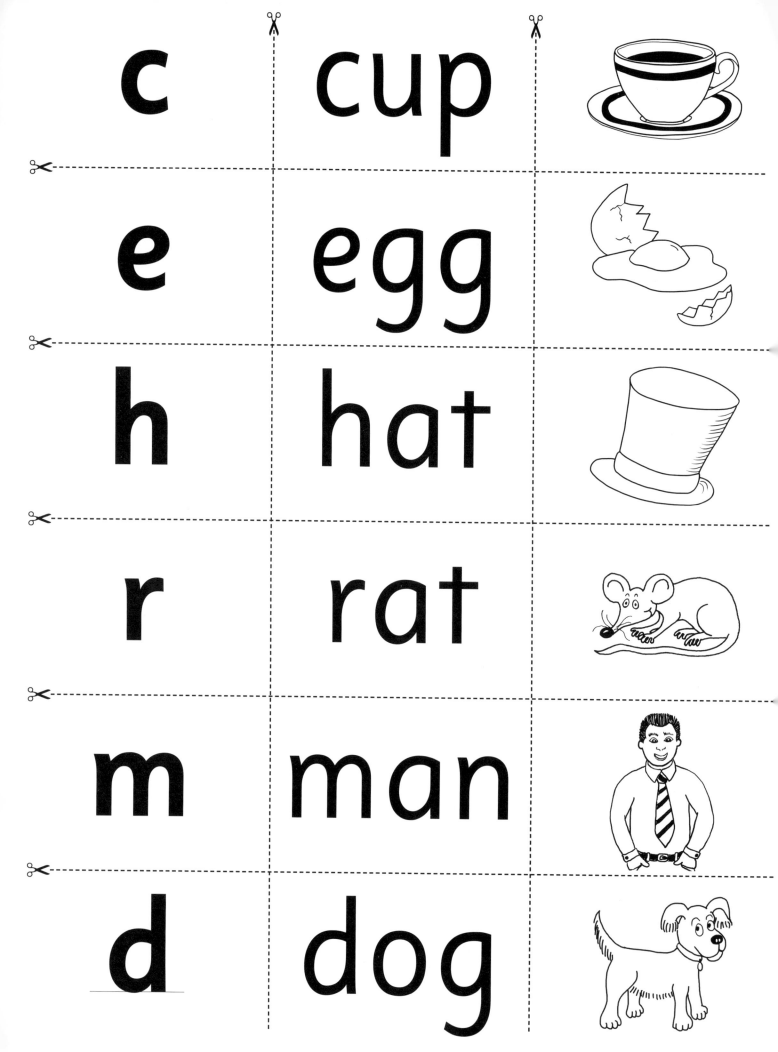
e	egg	
h	hat	
r	rat	
m	man	
d	dog	

g	goat	
o	octopus	
u	umbrella	
l	leg	
f	fan	
b	bed	

ai	rain	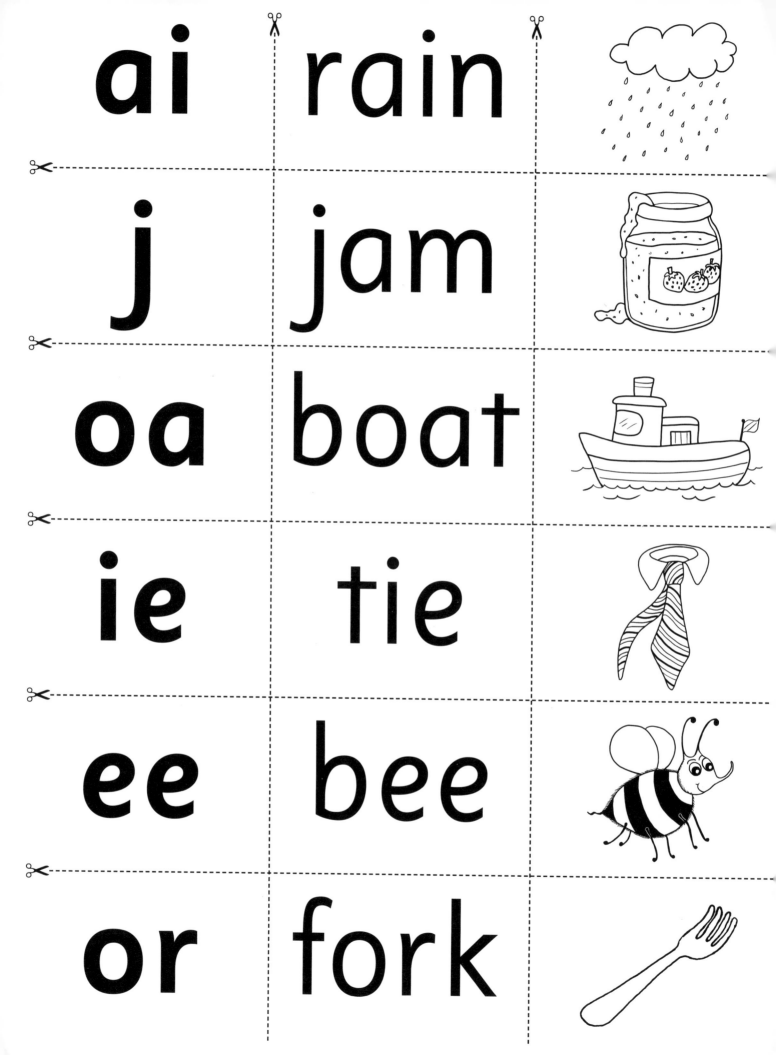
j	jam	
oa	boat	
ie	tie	
ee	bee	
or	fork	

z	zip	
w	web	
ng	ring	
v	van	
oo	book	
oo	moon	

y	yak	
x	fox	
ch	chick	
sh	ship	
th	feather	
th	moth	

qu	queen	
ou	cloud	
oi	oil	
ue	cue	
er	butter	
ar	car	

Sentence Pasting

Young students love cutting and pasting, and these sheets provide lots of blending practice in a fun, multisensory way. They can be used once the students have been taught the 42 letter sounds and the first twelve tricky words. Sentence pasting can be done as a craft activity, but the sentences and picture cards can also be prepared in advance, if preferred.

The students cut up the sentences, read them, and paste them under the correct pictures. Then they color the pictures on the sheet. All the sentences have regular words for the students to blend, except for the tricky words *I, the, he, she,* and *we.*

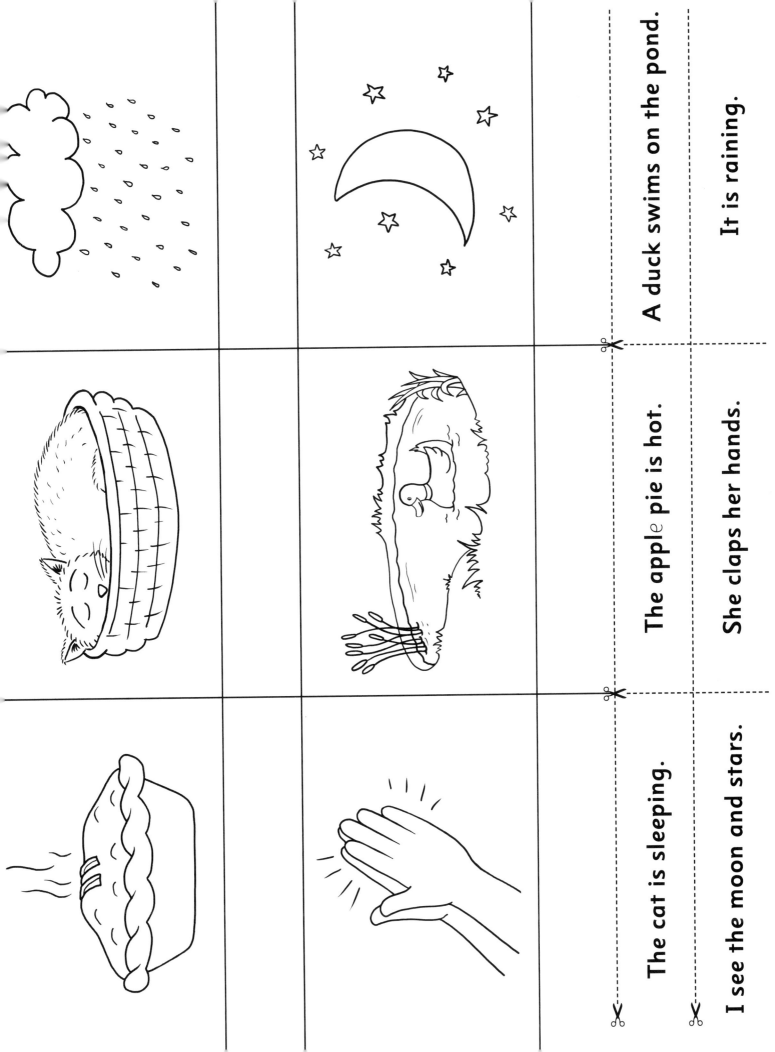

A duck swims on the pond.

It is raining.

The apple pie is hot.

She claps her hands.

The cat is sleeping.

I see the moon and stars.

The dog has black spots.

We had eggs for dinner.

I paint with a brush.

The bell is ringing.

I see an oak tree.

The letter has a stamp.

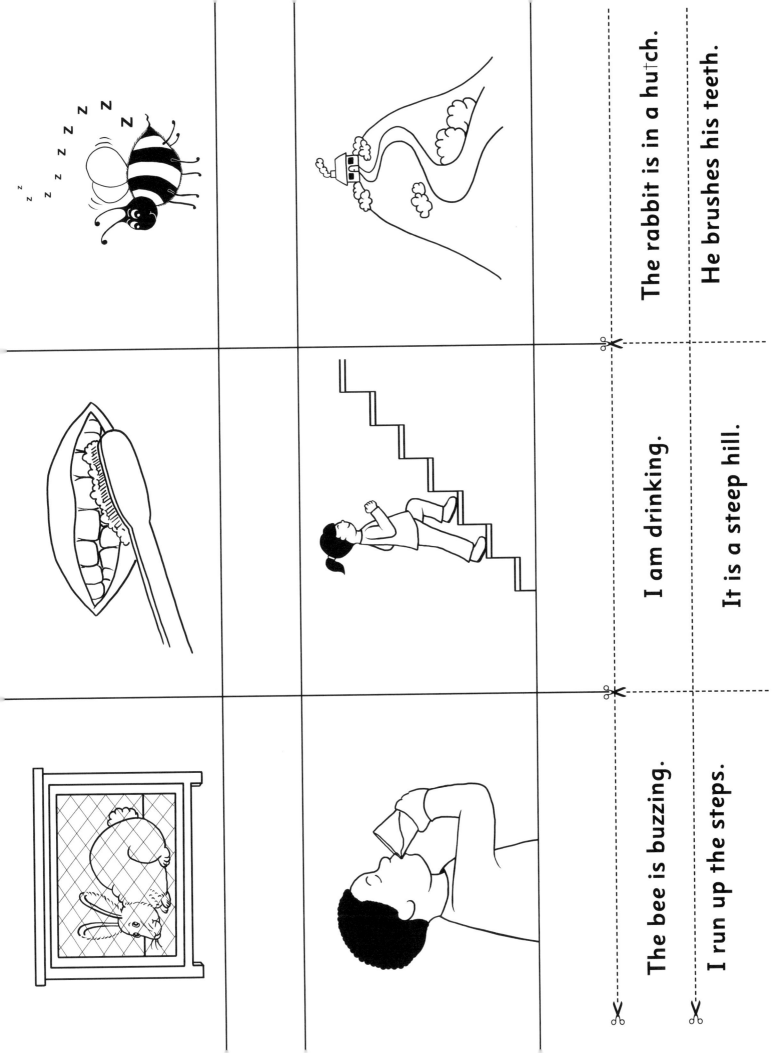

The rabbit is in a hutch.

He brushes his teeth.

I am drinking.

It is a steep hill.

The bee is buzzing.

I run up the steps.

Missing Sounds Sheets

Students learn to write independently by listening for the sounds in a word and writing the letters for those sounds. This skill needs to be developed gradually and the following activity sheets are designed to give this progression.

Each sheet has pictures with lines underneath. Each picture represents a word, and the lines represent the sounds in that word. Longer lines represent a digraph. The students listen for the sounds and write them on the lines. If this is too difficult, the letters could be written in beforehand, leaving just one to be filled in by the student.

Sheet 1: dog, bat, pen, net, cat, mug, six, sun, bed.
Sheet 2: star, fish, rain, pie, boat, oil, tree, moon, ring.
Sheet 3: hand, frog, tent, crab, plug, nest, drum, belt, flag.

_ _ _

_ _ _

_ _ _

_ _ _

_ _ _

_ _ _

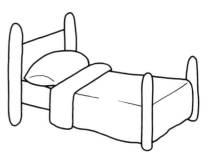

_ _ _

_ _ _

_ _ _

- - - - - -   - - - - - -   - - - - - -

- - - - - -   - - - - - -   - - - - - -

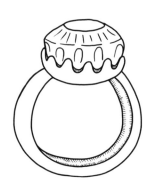

- - - - - -   - - - - - -   - - - - - -

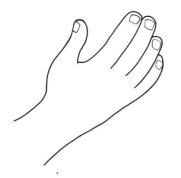

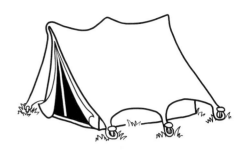

_ _ _ _ _

_ _ _ _ _

_ _ _ _ _

_ _ _ _ _

_ _ _ _ _

_ _ _ _ _

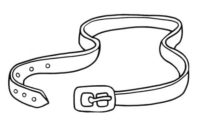

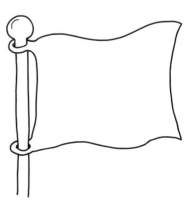

_ _ _ _ _

_ _ _ _ _

_ _ _ _ _

Homework Writing Sheets

About 40 percent of words can be spelled correctly by listening for the sounds and writing the letters that relate to those sounds. Students need to have plenty of practice sounding out and writing words, progressing to phrases and sentences. The homework writing sheets provide this practice and are a first step toward independent writing. Most students are ready to start toward the end of week ten and should be able to write a page on their own by the end of the first year. The sheets should only be used when a student has learned to identify the sounds in words and can write the letters for themselves. The aim is to develop fluency.

A set of sheets can be copied for each student with his or her name written at the bottom. Cut out the first section and send it home in a homework writing book, along with instructions asking the parents to dictate the words to their child (these are provided on page 149). When the book returns, the next section can be sent home. Alternatively, each section can be mounted onto numbered cards to be sent home and returned.

Most students bring the book back the next day, not because it is demanded but because they are enthusiastic. Not all the words have to be correct before sending home the next section, but any mistakes can be used to identify problems; perhaps the student has not listened to the sounds carefully enough or does not know how to write certain letters. As long as the student is coping quite well, (s)he can be given the next section.

The sheets start with simple, phonically regular, two- or three-letter words, which are followed by longer words with digraphs and consonant blends. Once the student is confident at writing words, the phrases can be used. Then, when the student knows and can spell the tricky words used, the sheets with sentences can be sent home.

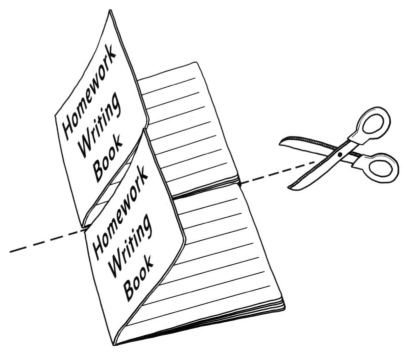

List 1	List 2	List 3
cat	cap	set
dog	dot	hit
dad	mat	it
red	tap	dip
top	did	mom
six	rot	bet
him	sat	yes
hat	pet	hut
sad	had	zip
hot	ram	lap

List 4	List 5	List 6
up	hid	van
let	hum	jug
rod	gun	in
hop	job	on
cot	fig	men
mud	win	bun
bed	not	leg
lid	sun	wet
bit	web	fun
bat	fog	peg

List 7	List 8	List 9
log	big	dug
jam	bag	mix
rug	ox	fed
net	am	din
lip	if	pop
tip	cod	bus
hug	bud	gas
got	gap	fix
dig	mug	pod
lot	an	nut

List 10	List 11	List 12
run	can	rub
bad	hen	man
get	fit	vet
jog	mad	cut
bug	ten	pan
met	pit	fat
lit	fox	map
pot	cup	rip
us	rat	rob
but	jet	pin

List 13

step
prod
damp
mist
lamp
test
spot
limp
slip
drum

List 14

list
west
dust
spit
mend
stop
jump
wind
clip
dump

List 15

bump
hunt
bent
hand
loft
spin
band
just
tent
drip

List 16

chin
trap
plum
lost
hush
snap
fresh
swum
long
split

List 17

film
then
grin
bang
cloth
gulp
bulb
sting
flat
blunt

List 18

smash
wing
bench
drop
stamp
trust
from
golf
bunch
thing

List 19	List 20	List 21
ship	snip	sand
fish	hung	crash
stand	wish	that
them	bend	this
bran	belt	song
chip	melt	land
shop	lump	quit
thump	went	dish
shelf	must	cash
pinch	lend	sang

List 22	List 23	List 24
rich	swing	crab
with	much	chop
chest	frog	swam
lunch	spend	shed
club	flash	glad
best	ring	shut
ramp	help	pant
flag	frost	soft
plug	thin	scrub
slept	slug	held

List 25	List 26	List 27
tie	bee	pie
rain	pain	paid
goat	road	aid
weep	sheep	teeth
oats	tied	feed
load	boat	toad
die	chain	died
seed	coat	quilt
raid	lie	coach
quiz	feet	meet

List 28	List 29	List 30
good	cue	out
moon	jar	cart
hook	boil	fern
wood	loud	fuel
food	mouth	oil
roof	coin	card
look	part	south
boot	farm	soil
wool	shout	sharp
soon	march	join

List 31

toast
cloud
born
paint
moist
scarf
broom
north
joint
short

List 32

train
spoil
start
found
storm
stood
spoon
fort
sweep
count

List 33

sweet
float
snort
snail
point
round
corn
smart
bloom
sport

List 34

magpie
winter
forget
longer
rooster
slither
artist
continue
toilet
zooming

List 35

sister
clever
nutmeg
singer
roast
rescue
morning
wigwam
boiling
street

List 36

proud
blister
number
torch
trumpet
roaming
argue
ointment
splash
liquid

List 37

a long scarf
boiling hot
a loud thump

List 38

a fish pie
hail and rain
a red hood

List 39

a zooming jet
sheep in a pen
a rushing river

List 40

a bad blister
never ending
a good cartoon

List 41

a hard winter
polishing boots
shout and argue

List 42

a shooting star
bats in a barn
a foolish jester

List 43

a bad throat
six magpies
a proud queen

List 44

a trip north
a gusting wind
up in a tree

List 45

a big statue
her big sister
a sharp point

List 46

a short quiz
gathering twigs
a silver spoon

List 47

a drifting ship
munching on a bun
a splendid outfit

List 48

a marching band
three sailing boats
a screech and a yelp

List 49

I was feeling hot.

Do not harm the robin.

The waiter brings us food.

List 50

Do not be sad for me.

That is the best thing to do.

The thunder was loud.

List 51

I can explain it all.

She can swim in the river.

It is not far to the bus stop.

List 52

We all tried the pie.

I must not argue with her.

He cut himself on a sharp nail.

List 53

The sheep are in the barn.

Dad needs to fix his car.

Sit on the bench with me.

List 54

Do not run into the road.

All the jam tarts are for me.

We can shelter in this shed.

List 55

Dad is painting the shelf.

I wish I had a good job.

The man had a scar on his chin.

List 56

The ship is sailing north.

We do not need his help.

She was a strong queen.

List 57

I can see a man with a hat.

He must wait for the next train.

It is freezing this morning.

List 58

She has a quilt on her bed.

The string is long and strong.

He found a coin on the ground.

List 59

Do not be such a spoilsport.

I was sleeping in the tent.

He swept the yard with a broom.

List 60

I found a cat in the farmyard.

She got a blister on her foot.

We are all having fish and chips.

Homework Writing Book: Parents' Advice Sheet

✂

Dear Parent,

Your child has been learning how to write by listening for the sounds in a word and writing the appropriate letter(s) for the sounds. Please help your child to practice these skills by calling out the words, phrases, or sentences provided, for your child to write as neatly as possible into the accompanying homework writing book. If your child is tired, do feel free to leave the homework until another time.

✂

Dear Parent,

Your child has been learning how to write by listening for the sounds in a word and writing the appropriate letter(s) for the sounds. Please help your child to practice these skills by calling out the words, phrases, or sentences provided, for your child to write as neatly as possible into the accompanying homework writing book. If your child is tired, do feel free to leave the homework until another time.

✂

Dear Parent,

Your child has been learning how to write by listening for the sounds in a word and writing the appropriate letter(s) for the sounds. Please help your child to practice these skills by calling out the words, phrases, or sentences provided, for your child to write as neatly as possible into the accompanying homework writing book. If your child is tired, do feel free to leave the homework until another time.

✂

Dear Parent,

Your child has been learning how to write by listening for the sounds in a word and writing the appropriate letter(s) for the sounds. Please help your child to practice these skills by calling out the words, phrases, or sentences provided, for your child to write as neatly as possible into the accompanying homework writing book. If your child is tired, do feel free to leave the homework until another time.

✂

Dear Parent,

Your child has been learning how to write by listening for the sounds in a word and writing the appropriate letter(s) for the sounds. Please help your child to practice these skills by calling out the words, phrases, or sentences provided, for your child to write as neatly as possible into the accompanying homework writing book. If your child is tired, do feel free to leave the homework until another time.

Tricky Words

When students start to write sentences, there are some frequently used words that they need to be able to use, such as *I, the, he, she, me, we, be, was, to, do, are,* and *all*. However, these words are tricky because the students cannot read or write them simply by using the sounds they have been taught so far. There are tricky parts that have to be learned, such as the alternative spellings for /ie/ in *my* and *like* or the irregular spellings in words like *said* and *two*.

When teaching a tricky word to the students, say the word and then blend the sounds, working out together which parts are regular and which are tricky. For example, when reading the word *said*, the /s/ and /d/ can be sounded out reliably, but the students will need to remember that the ‹ai› says the sound /e/. Working out these tricky parts and being made aware of any spelling patterns that the tricky words share, such as the letter ‹e› saying the sound /ee/ in *he, she, me, we,* and *be*, will help the students to remember the word.

The tricky words start being introduced when the students are learning the sixth letter-sound group, with *I* being taught alongside /sh/, followed by *the*, which is taught in the same lesson as the voiced /th/. The students learn how to read and write the tricky words at the same time, but it may take a while before the students are able to write them consistently with correct spelling.

The tricky words need plenty of practice and can be reviewed using the Jolly Phonics Cards or the Jolly Phonics Tricky Word Wall Flowers. Alternatively, the reproducible cards on pages 159 and 160 could be enlarged, cut out, and mounted onto card. The timetables on pages 4 to 6 show when to teach the tricky words across Steps 1 to 3.

The following activities are particularly useful for learning to spell tricky words.

1. Say as it sounds

Say the word as it should be pronounced according to its spelling. For example, when teaching the words *was* and *mother*, point out that the spellings say /w-a-s/ to rhyme with *mass* and /m-o-th-er/ to rhyme with *bother*. This technique is useful for learning any word with one element that makes it difficult to spell, such as *Wednesday* (Wed-**nes**-day) or *doctor* (doct**or**).

2. Word families or patterns

Point out words which share the same, or similar, spelling pattern. For example, the tricky words *he, she, me, we,* and *be* all have a single ‹e› making the /ee/ sound; *to* and *do* have a single ‹o› making the long /oo/ sound; *you* is at the beginning of *your*, and *any* is at the beginning of *many*; in *could, should,* and *would*, the ‹oul› makes the little /oo/ sound.

3. Look, copy, cover, write, check

First, the students look at the word and identify the tricky part. Then they write the word by copying it. Next they cover the word and try writing it again by themselves. Finally, they uncover the word and check whether it is correct, before covering it again and having another go.

4. Tricky word wall flowers

Inky Mouse has a tricky word hat to help her learn the tricky words. The tricky words are presented on six sets of flowers, with a different color for each set (blue, yellow, red, green, pink, brown). Build up the display as the tricky words are taught and use them regularly to review the tricky words.

5. Does it look right?

If students are not sure how to write the tricky part, they could try writing the word in different ways to see which one looks right. This works particularly well for tricky words that have an alternative vowel spelling, such as *my, by,* and *like*. For example, they could write down *my, mie,* and *migh* and then decide which one looks right.

6. Mnemonics

A few words are so irregular that it is difficult to remember how to spell them. Using mnemonics can be useful in these cases. Mnemonics are phrases in which the first letter of every word gives the spelling. A good example is "**b**ig **e**lephants **c**atch **a**nts **u**nder **s**mall **e**lephants" for the tricky word *because*. Another one is "**o u l**ucky **d**uck" for the common spelling pattern shared by *could, should,* and *would*.

Tricky word sheets

The flowers below and on the following page are to be copied, cut out, and used with the worksheets for tricky word sets 1 to 3 (pages 153 to 155). Each of these shows a tricky word hat with twelve tricky word flowers growing out of it. The students write over the dotted letters in the flowers and read the words. Then they read the words on the cut-out flowers and match them to the flowers on the tricky word hat.

The tricky words in sets 4 to 6 can be reviewed with the worksheets on pages 156 to 158. Here, the students write over the dotted letters in each flower to read the word. Then they find it in the wordsearch and join the two words together.

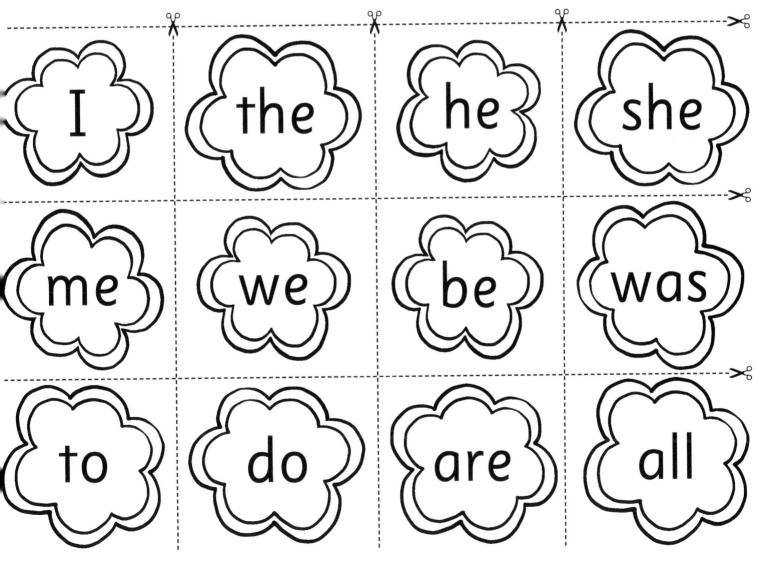

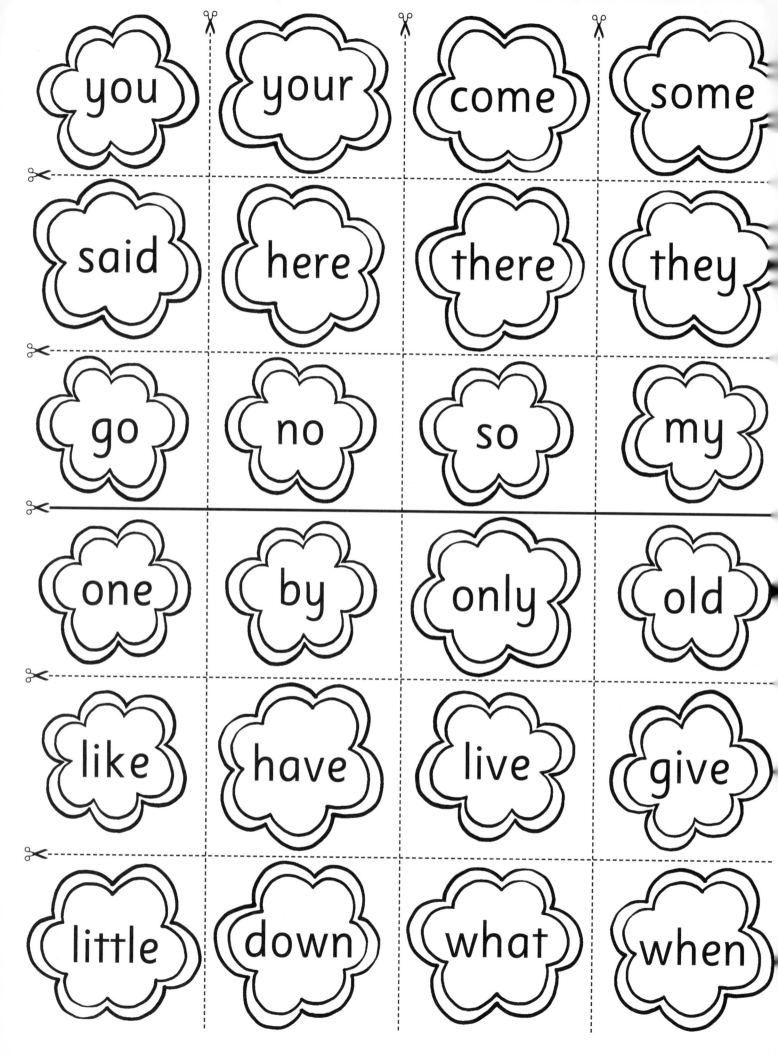

Write over the dotted letters and read the tricky words.

Write over the dotted letters and read the tricky words.

Write over the dotted letters and read the tricky words.

Write the words. Find the words. Join the words.

before

where

were

want

because

other

who

more

why

which

any

many

4

i	h	m	g	b	e	f	o	r	e
g	l	k	z	e	w	a	n	t	f
b	a	n	y	o	r	w	h	o	k
x	j	w	h	i	c	h	y	b	i
k	i	b	e	c	a	u	s	e	h
v	o	f	x	h	s	w	e	r	e
q	s	m	a	n	y	c	w	h	y
l	e	q	u	d	w	h	e	r	e
j	u	s	m	o	r	e	l	t	a
o	t	h	e	r	k	u	j	i	x

Write the words. Find the words. Join the words.

5

made

saw

their

does

could

two

should

four

put

would

goes

right

b	w	o	l	k	a	p	u	t	n
q	u	i	w	o	u	l	d	a	p
z	m	a	d	e	n	g	o	e	s
o	v	u	t	h	e	i	r	n	y
s	c	o	u	l	d	e	x	q	u
g	l	y	c	a	r	i	g	h	t
d	o	e	s	b	o	t	w	o	r
j	e	f	o	u	r	s	h	a	p
v	i	n	g	s	h	o	u	l	d
o	r	s	a	w	k	y	e	z	i

Write the words. Find the words. Join the words.

6

father   after   eight   mother

cover   upon   also   once

of   every   love   always

e	q	u	p	l	o	v	e	s	k
d	c	o	m	f	a	t	h	e	r
o	k	r	e	v	e	r	y	i	g
j	o	f	b	e	i	g	h	t	l
q	u	a	l	w	a	y	s	k	o
s	c	o	v	e	r	l	y	a	b
d	z	a	m	o	t	h	e	r	y
a	f	t	e	r	g	u	p	o	n
z	i	c	h	a	l	s	o	x	e
i	b	r	o	n	c	e	r	y	m

Tricky Words	Tricky Words	Tricky Words
I	you	one
the	your	by
he	come	only
she	some	old
me	said	like
we	here	have
be	there	live
was	they	give
to	go	little
do	no	down
are	so	what
all	my	when

Tricky Words	Tricky Words	Tricky Words
why	saw	once
where	put	upon
who	could	always
which	should	also
any	would	of
many	right	eight
more	two	love
before	four	cover
other	goes	after
were	does	every
because	made	mother
want	their	father

Alternative Spellings

By teaching one way to write the letter sounds initially, the students are given the ability to write independently. They listen for the sounds in a word and write down the letters for those sounds. However, once the students have learned the 42 letter sounds and can confidently blend and segment words using them, they need to be made aware of the alternative ways that some of the sounds, particularly the vowel sounds, can be written.

In Steps 2 and 3, the students are introduced to these alternative spellings, according to the scope and sequence mapped out in the timetables on pages 5 and 6. The students need to be given plenty of practice blending words with the alternative spellings. Sets of regular words can be made for each alternative – such as *snake, lake, bake, same, plate,* and *fame* for ‹a_e› and *may, pray, stay, lay, day, spray,* and *hay* for ‹ay›. Suitable words can be found in the Jolly Phonics Word Bank. The regular blending of words which use these alternatives helps the students become familiar with the spellings and enables them to cope with a wider range of words when reading. Students deal with the alternative spellings more easily for reading than for spelling, so students are not expected to use them consistently in their writing at this stage.

The following sheets for Steps 2 and 3 are provided in this section:

Sound sheets for the alternative spellings:	pages 162–187
Flashcards for the alternative spellings:	pages 188–191
Matching letters, words, and pictures:	pages 192–196

The alternative spellings need to be reviewed regularly over the next few years to help the students with both their reading and spelling. For accurate spelling, they need to make the right choice when deciding which alternative is needed to write a word like *snake*: should it be *snaik, snake, or snayk*? Being familiar with the alternatives will help them make the choice more easily. As the students become more widely read and familiar with words, the choice becomes easier still. Through their knowledge of sounds, and the letter patterns associated with them, the students' awareness of the details of spelling is heightened.

Sound sheet segmenting words

‹y› as /ee/	baby, cherry, teddy	‹ir›	girl, skirt, first
‹a_e›	cake, skate, whale	‹ur›	purse, yogurt, burger
‹e_e›	athlete, trapeze	‹ew›	ewe, skewer, pew
‹i_e›	bike, dice, slide	‹aw›	paw, straw, jigsaw
‹o_e›	bone, rose, globe	‹au›	launch, laundry, autumn
‹u_e›	cube, mule, perfume	‹al›	ball, chalk, wall
‹ay›	hay, tray, spray	‹ph›	photo, phone, graph
‹oy›	boy, oyster, cowboy	soft ‹c›	mice, pencil, cygnet
‹ea›	seal, peanut, beak	soft ‹g›	cage, magic, gymnast
‹y›	fly, spy, butterfly	‹air›	chair, fair, stairs
‹igh›	right, night, lighthouse	‹ear›	pear, bear, tear
‹ow› as /oa/	elbow, rainbow, window	‹are›	hare, square, share
‹ow› as /ou/	crown, cow, clown	long /oo/	glue, ruler, screw

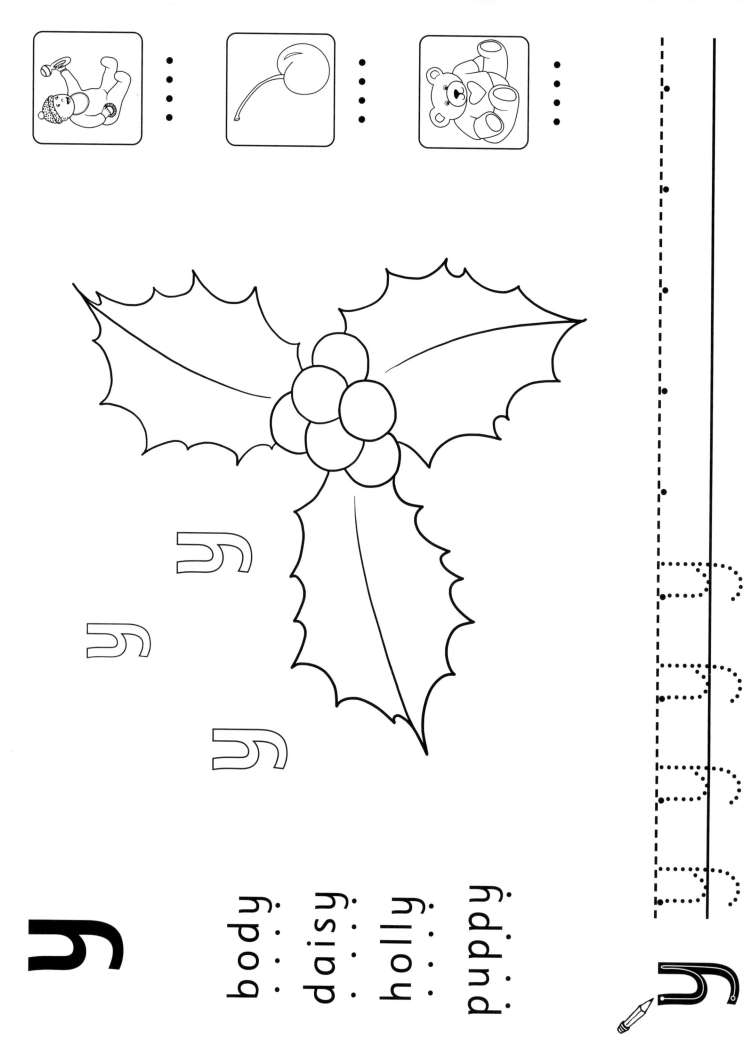

y

body
daisy
holly
puppy

a_e

gate : . . .
wave : . . .
game : . . .
snake : . . .

a_e

a_e

a_e

grapes cake

a_e

e_e

e_e   e_e

these
delete
trapeze
evening

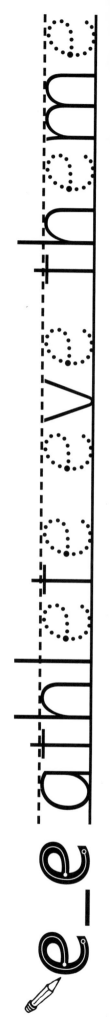

e_e athlete even theme

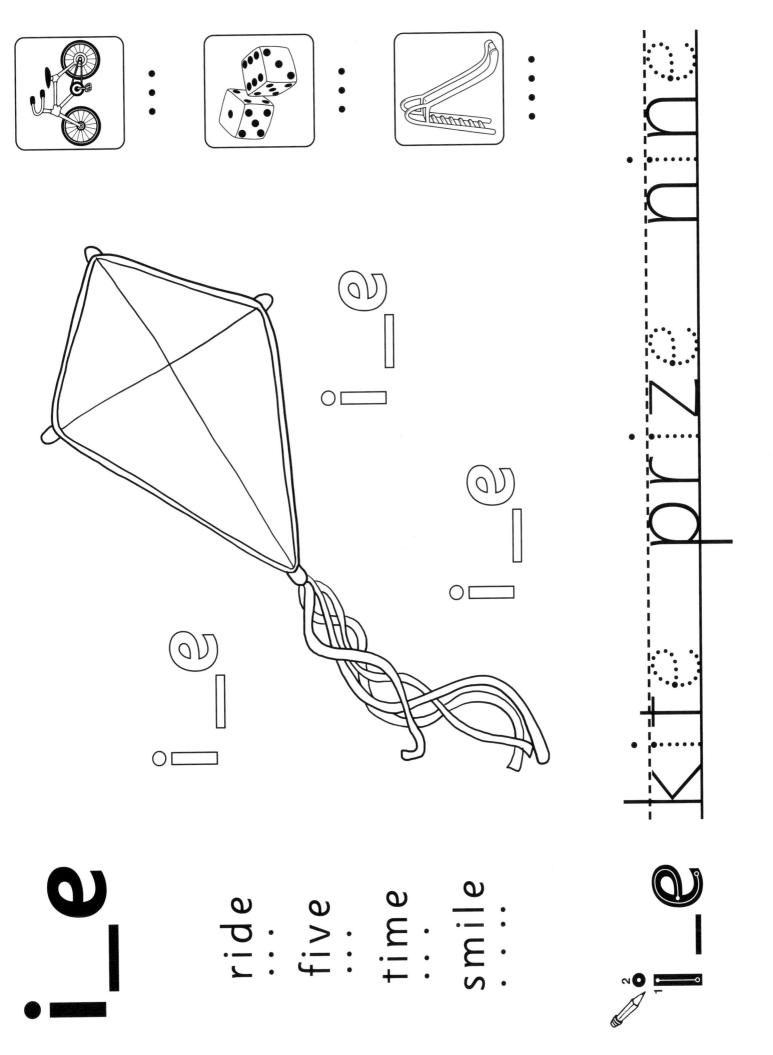

i_e

ride
five
time
smile

kite

prize

ki_e

pri_e

 :  :  : ⋮

o_e

joke : : :

note : : :

home : : :

stone : : : :

o_e

o_e

o_e

o_e

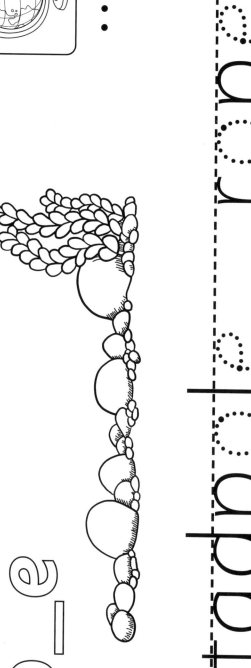

t a d p o l e

✏ o_e

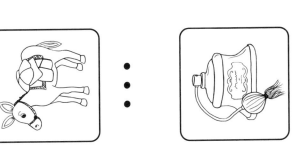

u_e

u_e · u_e · u_e

use :
cute : :
mule : :
fumes : :

cubes amuse

u_e

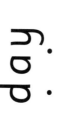
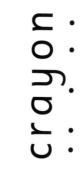

ay

ay

ay

ay

ay

day .
stay .
play .
crayon .

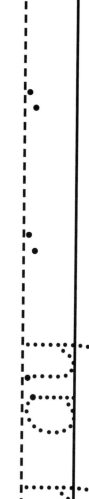

ay

oy

oy

oy

oy

toy .
joy .
annoy .
oyster .

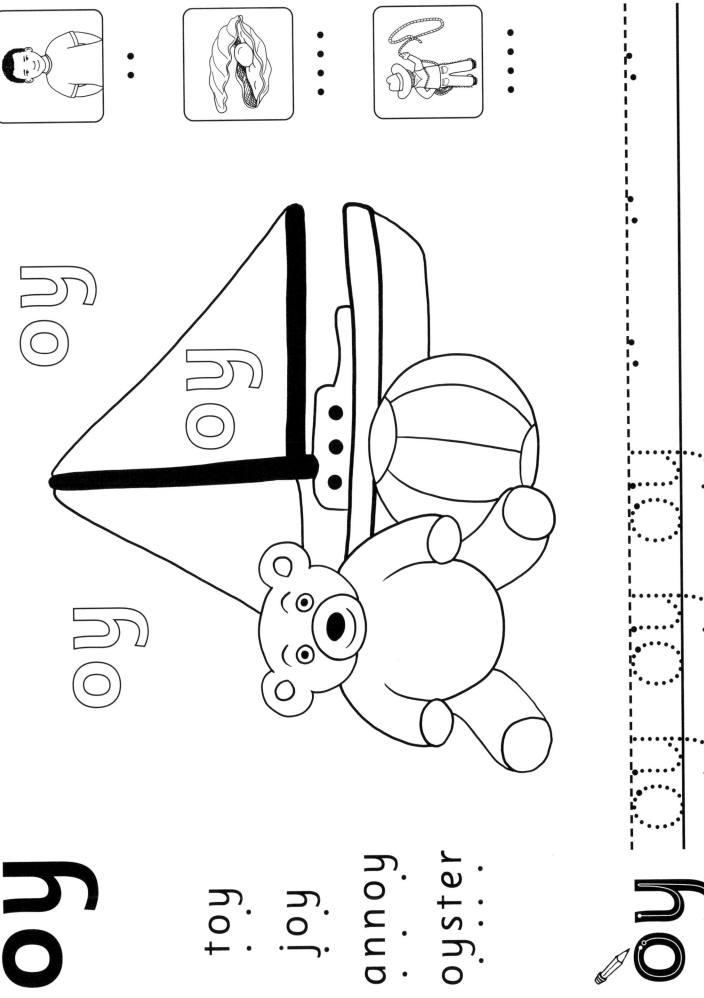

ea

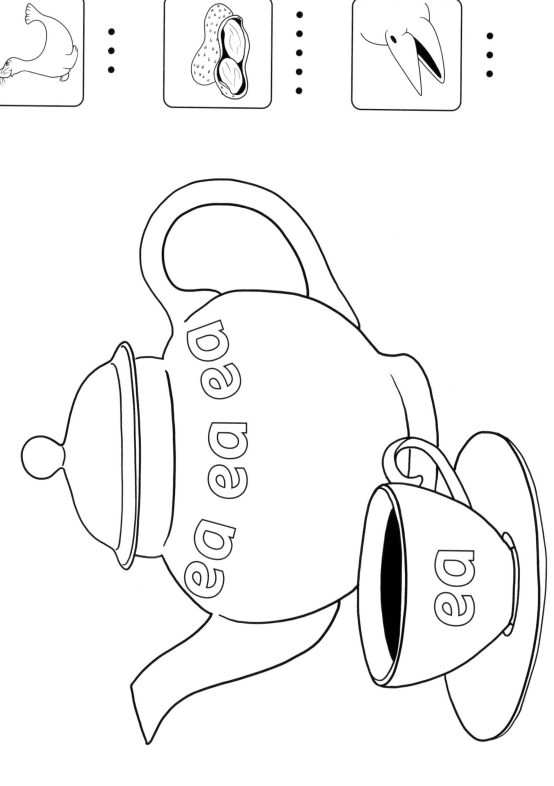

tea •
leaf •
peach •
seashell •

y

sky
dry
shy
reply

igh

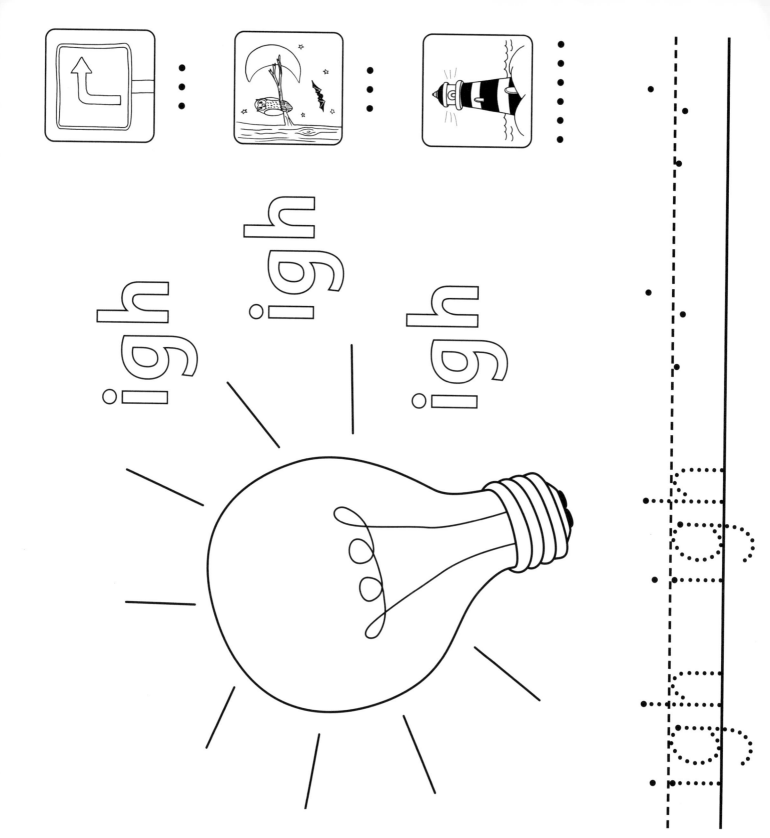

igh

igh

igh

igh

high ·
light ·
fight ·
bright ·

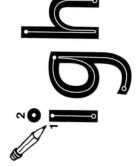

igh

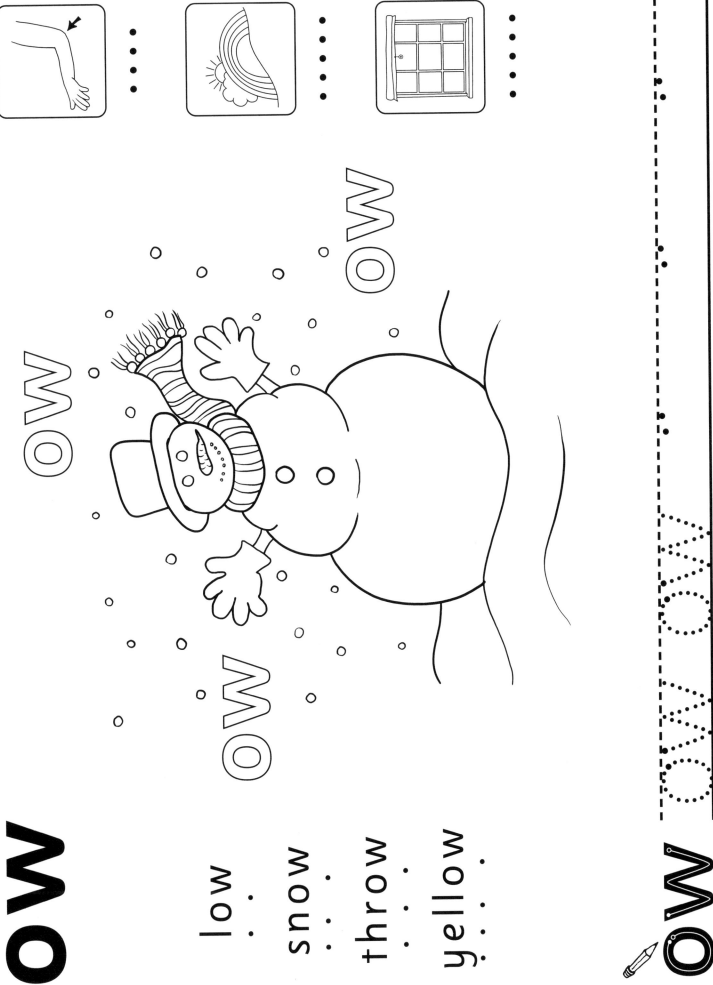

ow

ow

ow

ow

low ....
snow ....
throw ....
yellow ....

ow

ow

ow

ow

ow

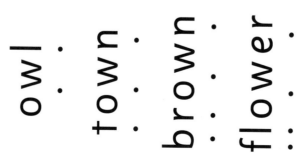

owl :
town :
brown :
flower :

ow ow ow

ir

ir

ir

ir

bird

dirt

stir

twirl

ur

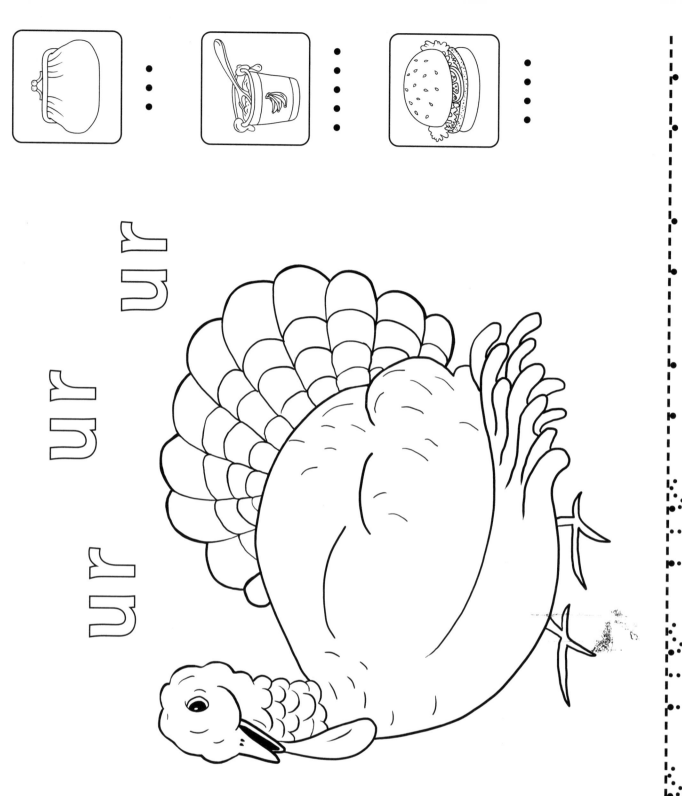

ur

ur ur

ur

fur :
curl :
hurt :
turn :

ur

ew

ew

ew

ew

ew

few .
fewer . .
skew . .
skewer . . .

ew

aw

saw
claw
draw
seesaw

aw

aw

aw

aw

au

au
au
au
au

haunt
launch
August
astronaut

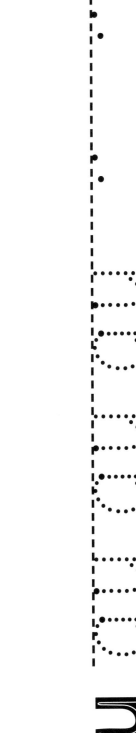

au

au

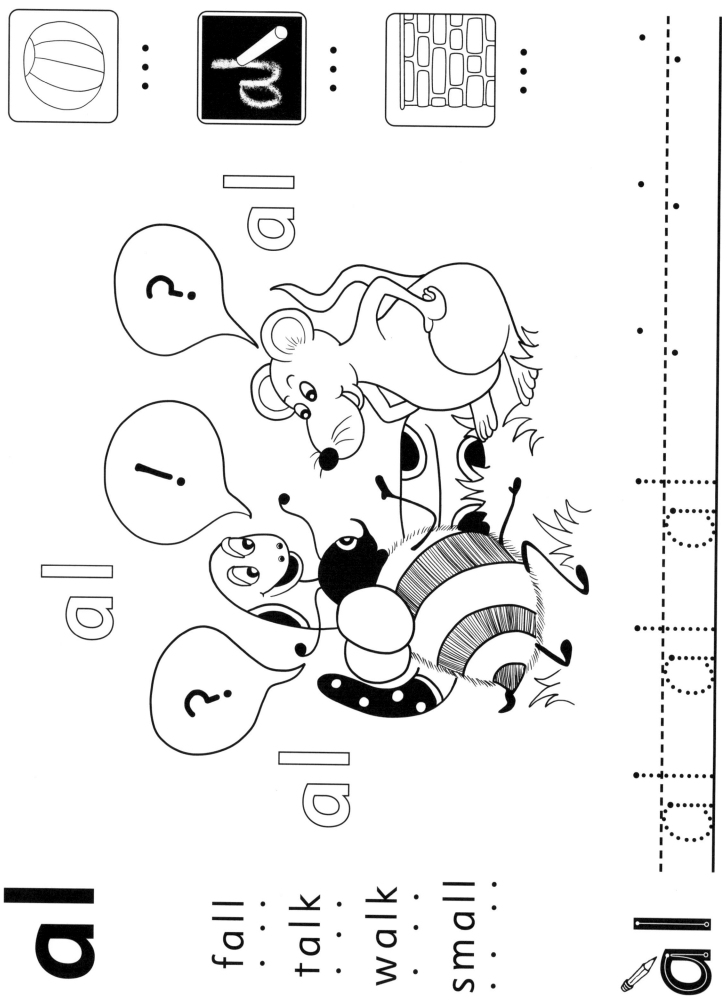

ph

ph

ph

ph

ph

dolphin

nephew

elephant

alphabet

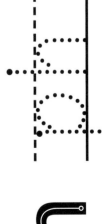

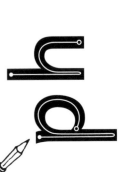

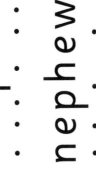
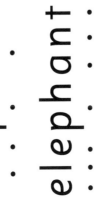

ph

soft c

face

fence

city

acid

bouncy

cycling

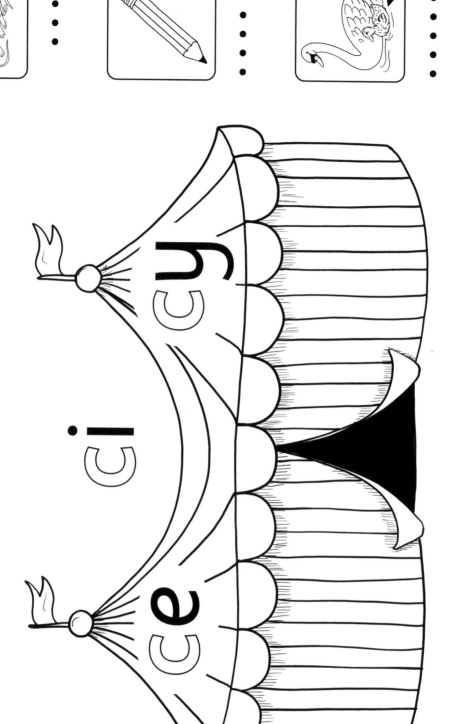

ci

cy

ce

 :

rice   fan   circus

soft g

ge gi gy

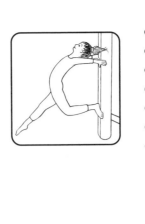

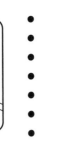

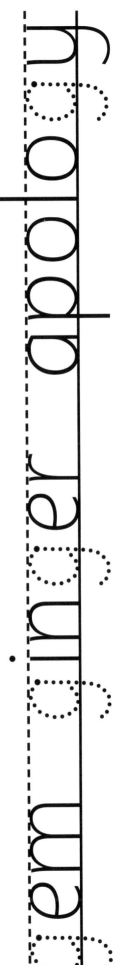

page

large

fragile

margin

dingy

energy

member ginger apology

air

air

air

air

air :
hair :
pair :
airport :

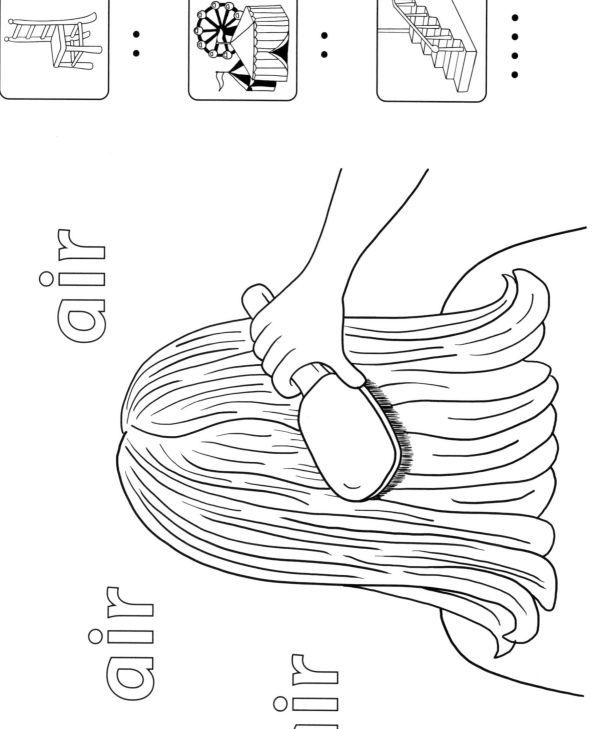

air

ear

ear

ear

b e a r .

t e a r .

p e a r .

w e a r .

: :

: :

: :

 ear

are

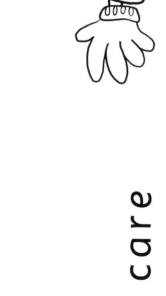 : 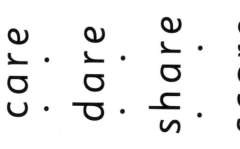 :  :

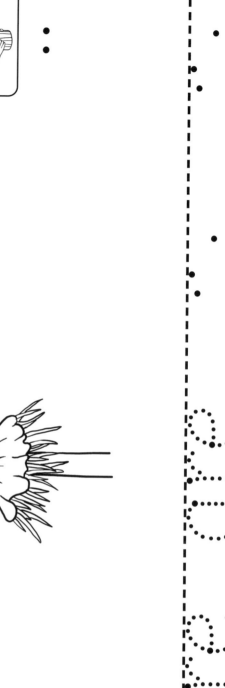

are

are

care ·
dare ·
share ·
scare ·

 are

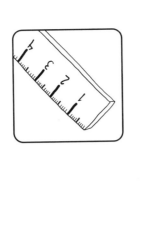

ue, u_e, ew as /oo/

ue

u_e

ew

blue ∴
true ∴
June ∴
flute ∴∴
chew ∴
jewel ∴

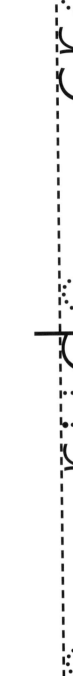

crew

rude

clue

a_e   ay

e_e   ea

i_e   igh

y　ck

o_e　ow

u_e　ew

ir   ur

oy   aw

au   al

c ^e_i_y

g ^e_i_y

ph

air

ear

are

a_e	gate
ay	hay
e_e	athlete
ea	leaf
i_e	kite
igh	light
y	fly

o_e	bone	
ow	snow	
u_e	cube	
ew	pew	
y	puppy	
k	king	
ck	duck	

oy	boy	
ow	owl	
ir	girl	
ur	purse	
aw	draw	
au	autumn	
al	ball	

ph	phone	
ce	mice	
ci	pencil	
cy	cycle	
ge	cage	
gi	magic	
gy	gymnast	

ue	glue	
u_e	ruler	
ew	jewel	
air	chair	
ear	pear	
are	hare	

Handwriting

In Step 1, the students are taught how to form the lower-case letters that represent the initial spellings of the 42 sounds. They feel the formation in the cut-out letter grooves of the Finger Phonics Books and practice writing the letters on their sound sheets. Giving the students a line to write on or using wide lined paper gives them something to aim for. It also helps develop both good handwriting and the students' fine motor skills.

In Step 2, the students review the formation of the lower-case letters, first by letter-sound group and then by common letter shapes. At the same time, they are taught how to form the capital letters. Capitals are the same size as tall letters, they start at or near the top, and they are never joined.

When reviewing lower-case formation, it is important to point out the following:

1. The bodies of all the letters should be the same size and should sit on the line.
2. The tall letters ‹b›, ‹d›, ‹f›, ‹h›, ‹k›, ‹l›, and ‹t› have a "stick" that goes up above the body. Letter ‹t› is slightly shorter than the other tall letters.
3. The letters ‹g›, ‹j›, ‹p›, ‹q›, and ‹y› have tails that go down below the line.
4. Most letters either start at or near the top and go down to the line, or start with a caterpillar /c/ as in ‹a›, ‹d›, ‹o›, ‹g›, and ‹q›.
5. The exceptions are ‹e›, which starts halfway up the letter, and ‹z›, which starts at the top, but goes along to the right before coming down to the line.

Letter formation, both lower- and upper-case, is also reviewed in the students' alphabet work in Step 2. In Jolly Phonics, the alphabet is divided into four color-coded groups: A–E (red), F–M (yellow), N–S (green), and T–Z (blue). This represents roughly the four quarters of a dictionary. Knowing which quarter a letter belongs to, will make it easier for students to look up words in a dictionary later on. When the students learn the alphabet, they learn the letter names, but they also need to remember the sound a capital makes and which lower-case letter it is paired with. The sheets on pages 198 to 206 can be used to practice the handwriting skills taught in Step 2.

In Step 3, the students continue to practice the formation of the capital letters and digraphs. By being fussy about pencil hold and correct formation from the beginning, bad habits are prevented. It will also ensure that the students develop neat and fluent handwriting and will give them a pride in their work.

Write these lower-case letters and their capitals.

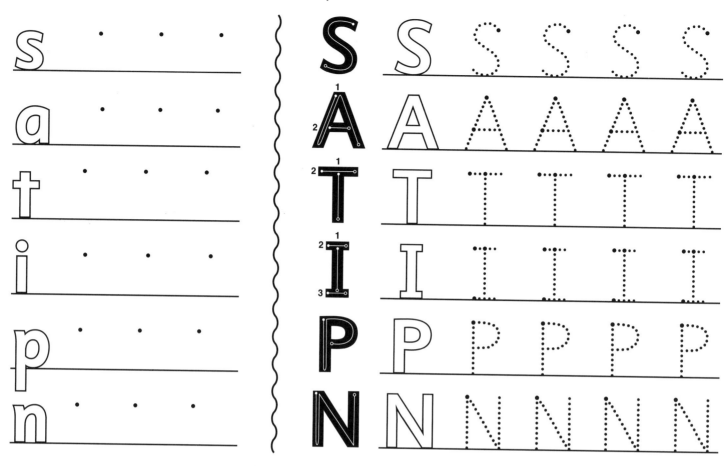

Write inside the outline letters and match the capital letters to the lower-case letters.

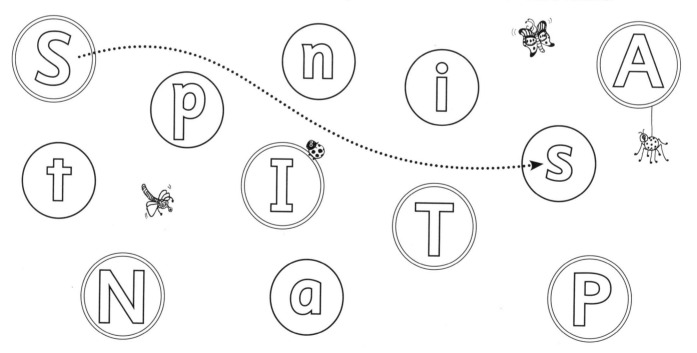

Write the capital letter for each of these lower-case letters.

Write these lower-case letters and their capitals.

c _____ C C C C C C

k _____ K K K K K K

e _____ E E E E E E

h _____ H H H H H H

r _____ R R R R R R

m _____ M M M M M M

d _____ D D D D D D

Write inside the outline letters and match the capital letters to the lower-case letters.

R   m   E   M

e   c   K

C   h   D   r   d

k   H

Write the capital letter for each of these lower-case letters.

e ___   k ___   r ___   d ___   h ___   m ___

Write these lower-case letters and their capitals.

g

o

u

l

f

b

G G G G G G

O O O O O O

U U U U U U

L L L L L L

F F F F F F

B B B B B B

Write inside the outline letters and match the capital letters to the lower-case letters.

Write the capital letter for each of these lower-case letters.

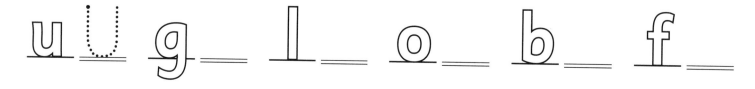

u U   g ___   l ___   o ___   b ___   f ___

Write these lower-case letters and their capitals.

j

z

w

v

y

x

q

J J j j j j j

Z Z z z z z z

W W w w w w w

V V v v v v v

Y Y y y y y y

X X x x x x x

Q Q q q q q q

Write inside the outline letters and match the capital letters to the lower-case letters.

Z   q   V   Q   X

V   x   w   j

Y   z   J   y   w

Write the capital letter for each of these lower-case letters.

v ___   j ___   x ___   q ___   z ___   y ___

Write inside the lower-case letters and join them to the matching capital letters.

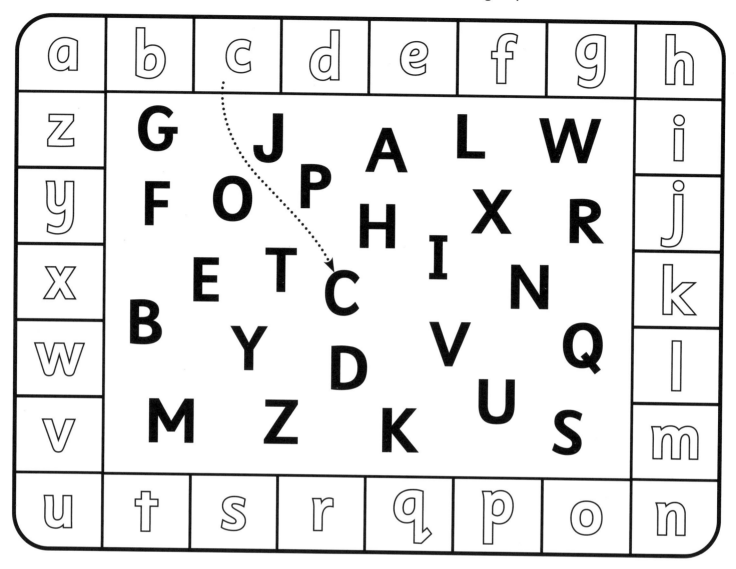

a	b	c	d	e	f	g	h

z · G J A L W · i

y · F O P X R · j

x · E T H I · k

w · B C V N Q · l

v · Y D U · m

· M Z K S ·

| u | t | s | r | q | p | o | n |

Write the capital letter next to each lower-case letter.

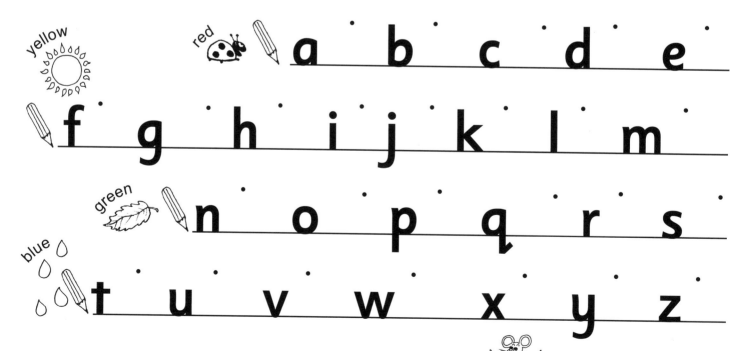

yellow

red a b c d e

f g h i j k l m

green n o p q r s

blue t u v w x y z

Can you say the alphabet?

Write inside the capital letters and join them to the matching lower-case letters.

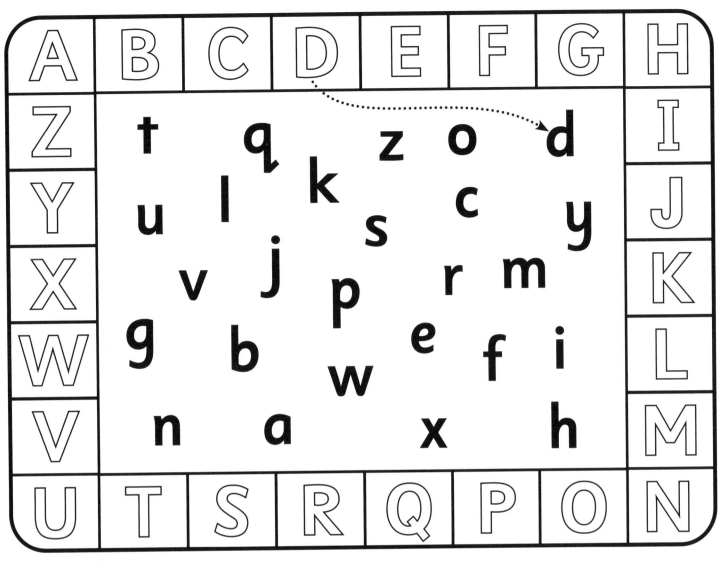

Write the lower-case letter next to each capital letter.

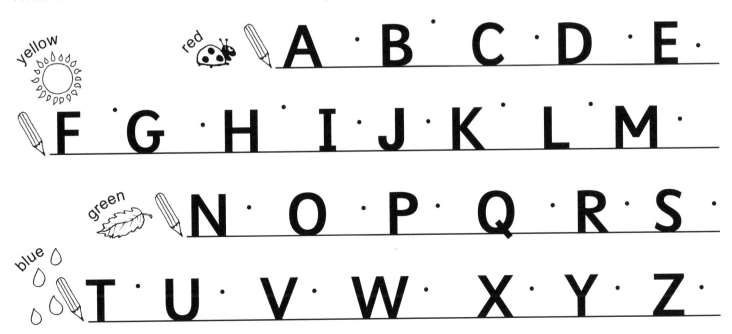

Can you say the alphabet without looking at it?

Practice writing these caterpillar /c/ letters.

c c c c c c c . . . . .

a a a a a a a . . . . .

d d d d d d d . . . . .

o o o o o o o . . . . .

g g g g g g g . . . . .

q q q q q q q . . . . .

Complete the alphabet, using the correct color for each section.

red
___ ___ ___ C ___ E

yellow
___ ___ G ___ ___ I J ___ ___ ___ M

green
N ___ ___ P ___ ___ ___ S

blue
___ ___ ___ U ___ ___ ___ ___ Y ___

Practice writing these tall letters.

b b b b b b
d d d d d d
h h h h h h
k k k k k k
l l l l l l
f f f f f f

Complete the alphabet, using the correct color for each section.

red

__ __ B __ D __

yellow

F __ __ H __ __ __ K L __

green

__ __ O __ __ Q R __

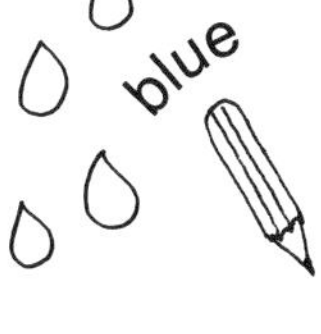

blue

T __ __ V __ __ X __ __ __

Practice writing these letters, which have tails that go under the line.

g g g g g g

j j j j j j

p p p p p p

q q q q q q

y y y y y y

Can you write the alphabet? Remember to use the correct color for each section.

yellow

red

green

blue

Guided Writing

Once the students know the letter sounds and are able to do simple dictation in their homework writing books, they are ready for some guided writing. While some students are able to write independently at an early age, most students need plenty of help and guidance. In the Words and Sentences lessons for Step 2, the students are given a writing topic and a model sentence to work on as a class. This gives them the initial support they need and introduces them to some basic sentence structure.

On the following pages there are thirteen pictures that can be used to start a class discussion. From this, the teacher chooses some key words and looks at how to spell them, pointing out any alternative spelling patterns or tricky words. Then the teacher writes the model sentence on the board and discusses it with the students, reminding them of the following: that sentences always start with a capital letter; that capital letters are always tall; to listen for the sounds in a word to write it; to write the letters close together, but without bumping; to leave a space between each word; that *I, the, are, he, to,* and *we* are tricky words; and not to forget the period at the end. Once the sentence has been discussed, the students copy it down and those who can already write independently should be encouraged to write a few sentences of their own. The students are not yet expected to use the alternative vowel spellings in their writing so their spelling will not always be accurate but it should be readable. By the end of the year, virtually every student should be writing independently, especially if they have spoken English.

Model Sentence

	Model Sentence
1. The hen	A hen just sits on her nest.
2. In the park	I can see a big dog.
3. On the pond	A boat sails on the pond.
4. The fox	The fox looks up at the moon.
5. The fish	That fish has a long tail.
6. In the dark	The moth is on the tree.
7. The noisy ducks	The ducks on the pond are quacking.
8. The queen	The queen has a red cloak.
9. Digging for gold	He went south and then north.
10. The shark in the ship	The strong shark swam in and around the ship.
11. Fixing the car	He helps to check the oil in the car.
12. The statue	The statue has a hat and coat.
13. Having a picnic	We had a picnic in the woods.

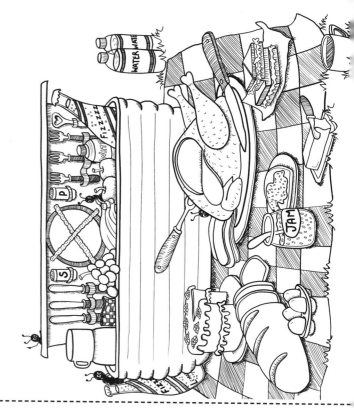

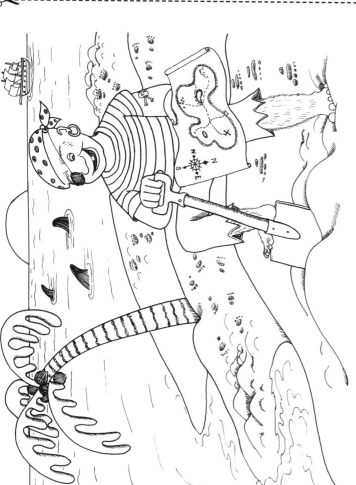
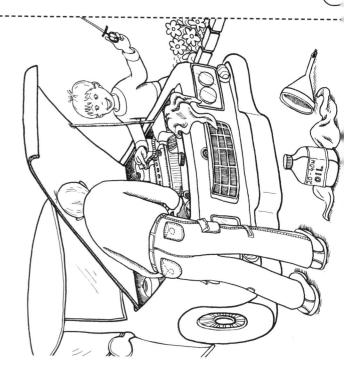

Reading Comprehension

Once the students are confident readers who are fluent at blending new words, the teaching can concentrate on other important skills, such as reading comprehension. For reading to be a meaningful activity, the students need to understand what it is they are reading.

Comprehension depends to some extent on the students' vocabulary, which is why vocabulary and comprehension should be taught from the beginning. In the early stages, these skills are taught aurally. The students listen to nursery rhymes, poems, and stories and are encouraged to talk about what happens and to answer simple comprehension questions. Then, once the students are blending unfamiliar words fluently, regular reading develops vocabulary and exposes the students to a wider range of words than they would meet every day in spoken language.

In Step 3, reading comprehension can be developed through the various activities provided on the following pages. The students respond to what they are reading by following instructions, drawing pictures, reading and answering questions, filling in missing words, matching, and working out simple clues.

Discuss each activity with the students first and encourage them to think about the text and what it is telling them. Point out the tricky words and alternative spellings, as well as any other words that are harder to work out, such as *water* and *find*. Although *water* is not regular, the students can try blending it and decide whether it sounds right – it is close enough that the adjustment can be made with a little encouragement – and *find* can be worked out using the following blending tip: If the short vowel does not work, try the long one.

Most of the comprehension activities are very straightforward but some need a little care; it is important to do the crossword on page 222 as a whole-class activity first, working out the answers (1. map, 2. doctor, 3. ant, 4. tent, 5. soap, 6. snake, 7. winter, 8. egg, 9. hand, 10. rock, 11. green, 12. dark) and giving guidance on the spelling for *egg, snake, rock, doctor,* and *dark.* The story of The Bad-Tempered Goat on page 221 could be told to the students beforehand, either in the teacher's own words or by reading the version in the Jolly Phonics Readers (Green Level).

These activities are the culmination of the teaching in Jolly Phonics as they allow the students to use all the skills they have been taught so far.

Out at Sea

 Add six fish.

 Add a big crab.

 Add a starfish.

 Add a boat.

 Add three red shells.

 Add a flying seagull.

 Add a shark with big teeth.

 Add a man in the boat.

 Add a yellow sun in the sky.

Yes or No?

Can snails jump? _____

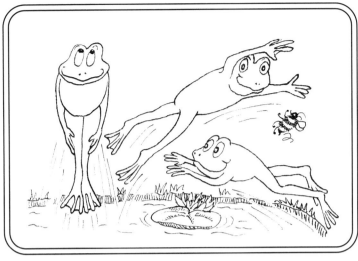

Can frogs hop? _____

Can ducks quack? _____

Do moths sing? _____

Is sand green? _____

Is the sun hot? _____

At the Park

1. The dog is carrying a _____.   stick / stone

2. There is a cat in the _____.   boat / tree

3. The fox is looking at the _____.   cat / rabbit

4. The ducks _____ on the pond.   quack / quit

5. The boys have a bat and _____.   ball / wall

6. The bird in the tree is _____.   singing / swinging

Read and Match

 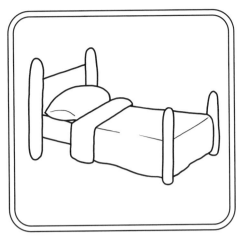 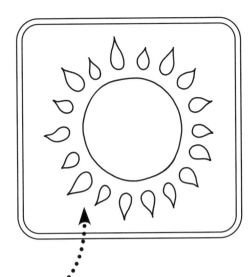

The sun is hot.

I sleep in a bed.

The boat is sailing.

The soap is on the dish.

This sock is long.

She is running.

 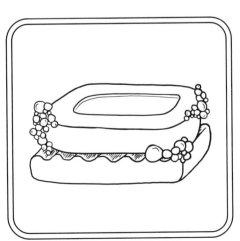 

Read and Draw

The rabbit lives
in a hutch.

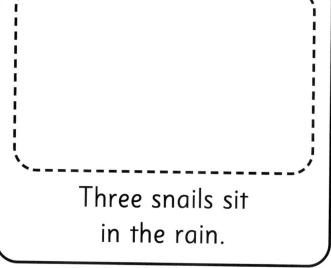

Three snails sit
in the rain.

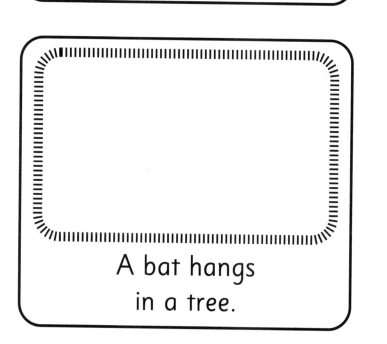

A bat hangs
in a tree.

There is a big
rainbow in the sky.

The moon and stars
shine brightly.

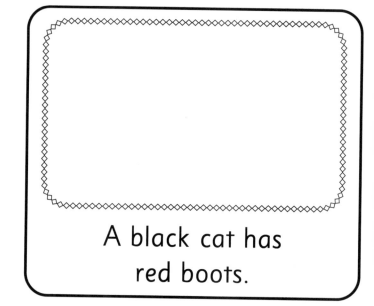

A black cat has
red boots.

Sentence Matching

I can see a hen. ●   ○ He likes to hop.

The oak tree is tall. ○   ○ He has big horns.

The goat is running. ○   ○ It has a brown shell.

A frog is in the pond. ○   ○ They have a bucket.

A snail sits in the rain. ○   ○ Its leaves are green.

The boys play in the sea. ○   ● Her beak is yellow.

Read, Write, and Color

 The tall oak _____ is green.

My _____ is long. It has red and black stripes.

 My brown _____ has a big collar.

The little green _____ jumped into the pond.

 The _____ shines in the night.

I found a _____ in the garden. It had a yellow shell on its back.

In the Zoo

1. How many monkeys are in the tree? _____

2. Which animal has a trunk? _____

3. What is the tall bird called? _____

4. Where is the crocodile swimming? _____

5. Who has black and white stripes? _____

6. How many giraffes are there? _____

Make as many words as you can from the letters in the word:

elephants

sleep

_____

_____

_____

_____

_____

_____

Having a Party

We had a party for _____

We ate some _____

_____

_____

_____

_____

The Bad-Tempered Goat

farmer
chickens
goat
sack
angry
tree
tractor
flies

On Moat Farm there are rabbits, cows, _____, some horses, and a goat.

The _____ has a very bad temper.

One morning, the _____ feeds his animals.

He gives the goat some oats from a big _____.

A cheeky robin sees the oats. He takes a quick peck and _____ up into the old oak tree.

The goat is _____ and butts the tree trunk very hard.

Crack, creak, crunch! The _____ falls on the goat.

The farmer gets his _____ and drags away the tree. The goat is free!

Crossword Clues

1. This will help you to find your way.
2. If you are ill, you go to see the _____ .
3. This small insect lives in a nest underground.
4. If you go camping, you may sleep in this.
5. You wash with _____ and water.
6. This animal hisses.
7. The time of year when it is cold.
8. A chick hatches from this.
9. This is on the end of your arm.
10. A very big stone.
11. The sky is blue and the trees are _____ .
12. At night it is _____ .

ant
hand
doctor
tent
egg
soap

map
winter
green
snake
rock
dark

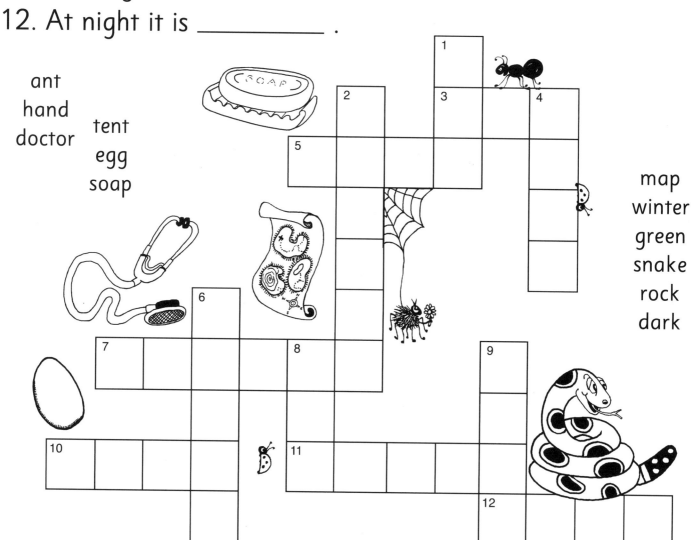

On the Beach

1. What are the children doing on the rocks?

_____

2. What can you see in the tide pool?

_____

3. What is on the top of the sandcastle?

_____

4. How many legs does an octopus have?

_____

5. How many beach umbrellas are there?

_____

6. What sort of animal is a seagull?

_____

The Midnight Feast

Once upon a time, there was a king called Alfred. His wife was Queen Matilda. They lived in a castle with a cat called Fluffy. One night, King Alfred was hungry. So he got up and made himself some cheese sandwiches to eat. Some crumbs from the sandwich fell onto the floor.

A mouse saw the crumbs from her mouse hole in the corner of the room. She could have a midnight feast if she was quick and quiet. She crept out and had just reached the crumbs, when Fluffy looked into the room.

The mouse ran for her hole as quickly as she could. Fluffy ran for the mouse as quickly as he could. The mouse reached her hole. She was hungry, but safe!

1. What is the king's name? _____

2. What is the queen's name? _____

3. What sort of animal is Fluffy? _____

4. What did King Alfred make to eat? _____

5. Who saw the crumbs on the floor? _____

6. Who saw the mouse? _____

7. Did the cat catch the mouse? _____